T0381155

The Warriors Way

Ultimate book of Netball sessions

Samantha Griffin

AuthorHouse™ UK
1663 Liberty Drive
Bloomington, IN 47403 USA
www.authorhouse.co.uk
UK TFN: 0800 0148641 (Toll Free inside the UK)
UK Local: 02036 956322 (+44 20 3695 6322 from outside the UK)

Because of the dynamic nature of the Internet, any web addresses or links contained in
this book may have changed since publication and may no longer be valid. The views
expressed in this work are solely those of the author and do not necessarily reflect the views
of the publisher, and the publisher hereby disclaims any responsibility for them.

Any people depicted in stock imagery provided by Getty Images are models,
and such images are being used for illustrative purposes only.
Certain stock imagery © Getty Images.

This book is printed on acid-free paper.

ISBN: 978-1-7283-5628-0 (sc)
ISBN: 978-1-7283-5627-3 (e)

Print information available on the last page.

Published by AuthorHouse 11/24/2020

authorHOUSE®

The
Warriors
Way

Contents

Strategies Part 3 97

Essentials 119

About the Author

I first discovered netball at primary school in Leicestershire. I started coaching at the age of 15 as a volunteer at my local club, and my passion for the sport has continued to grow. Since then I have always been determined to develop performance netball in my home region to offer opportunities to all. I am currently head coach of Charnwood Rutland Netball Club and U19 Loughborough Lightning Head Coach.

After six years of teaching PE, I set up a coaching business with my sister, Athletic Performance Coaching, which specialises in helping athletes reach their full potential across a number of different sports, including netball.

About the book

As a teacher and a coach, I found it challenging to gain access to innovative new drills that I could work into the different stages of a season.

So, I started writing this book to better support my team of coaches. I hope this book can help other coaches and teachers by providing ideas of how to achieve different targets each week, whatever level they are working at.

This book contains full session plans that you can follow or adapt to suit your group. The sessions are broken into stages that are intended to fit around natural breaks in the year. Each session aims to increase player's knowledge and understanding of the game and apply new strategies and tactics for attacking and defending during game situations. Ensure you consider what you want to achieve from your sessions to find and adapt appropriate plans from this book.

I believe that warm-ups are an important part of each session that players can lead. Once my players fully understand what I expect from a warm-up each week, I encourage different players to lead them to help promote strong leadership and decision-making across the whole team. Figure out what your expectations are and build them into your sessions to develop your players as a fully functioning team. Set your standards high, work hard and you will create a successful environment. These sessions have helped me to develop an entire club and achieve national success – I hope this book helps you achieve your goals too.

Key:
F = Feeder
A = Attacker (Purple)
D = Defender (Green)
-----= Path of the ball
CPs = Coaching points
▲ = Cone

Coaching Expectations

Be Professional

- Always be on time
- Take a register
- Wear appropriate kit
- Ensure sessions are planned
- Equipment is ready and checked

Create a positive environment

- Encourage communication, get athletes talking to each other
- Be approachable
- Make the session fun
- Ensure the session is safe
- Establish a supportive learning culture
- Provide feedback
- Celebrate success

High expectations

- Set goals
- Plan and delivery sessions that support learning
- Motivate and encourage all to be the best they can
- Ensure the session flows, progress drills
- Set the intensity of the session
- Work to achieve session aims
- Provide successful communication
- Set your own Non-negotiables

Attacking

Key: Possession

Passing/Ball Handling

Aim: For all players to understand and apply the correct technique for each pass.

Warm up: All players have a netball or tennis ball moving around within the court. When the coach shouts numbers the players apply the action, coach will also call a change in dynamic movement:

1. Throw the ball up and clap 3x before catching
2. Move the ball around the body whilst moving
3. Figure of 8 with the ball between the legs
4. Find a partner and make 5 passes, communicate who passes over/chest

Agility/Fitness: In pairs player 'A' passes the ball against the wall, whilst player 'B' completes sprint work for 1min, then change. Complete with all 5 of the below passes:

1. Right hand shoulder pass: CPs, start with the ball on right hand opposite ear, left hand supports the front, left leg steps, follow through the pass with right hand fingers finishing where you want the ball to go.
2. Left hand shoulder pass: CPs, start with the ball on left hand opposite ear, right hand supports the front, right leg steps, follow through the pass with left hand fingers finishing where you want the ball to go.
3. Chest pass: CPs, 'W' shape behind the ball, step in, push the ball from the chest to opposite players chest, ball travels flat and hard.
4. Over-head: Start with the ball above your head with two hands, step in and push the ball flat and hard.
5. Chest to over: CPs, transition release points from chest to above the head.

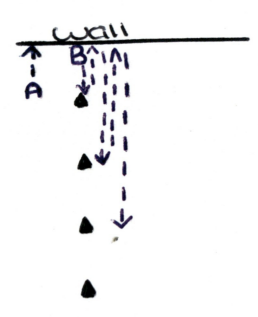

Samantha Griffin

Ball Placement: Clockwork

In pairs player 'A' drives to each cone to receive the ball, must return to the middle each time and change direction. Player 'B' uses chest pass, shoulder pass, overhead to deliver a pass depending on distance. 'A' works clockwise first change roles and repeat anti-clockwise.

CPs, 'A' Drive at speed, hands out in front, keeping body open to ball, land on the inside leg 'B' Feeder varies the pass depending on the distance, time the pass so 'A' not waiting, deliver the ball in front.

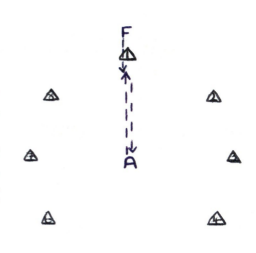

Progressions

1. 'B', Feeder calls number for 'A' to move to
2. Add a defender

Conditioned Game: Box Ball

Two teams, each team trying to score by catching the ball in a box. Only one player from the attacking team aloud in the box for a max of 5 seconds, defenders not allowed in the box. Cannot score in the same box twice in a row. If defence intercept they become attackers. First team to 10 points wins. Discuss in teams/repeat.

CPs, Driving into space, Communication

Question: What passes were successful when feeding into the box? Why?

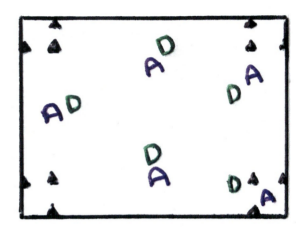

Progression:

1. Everyone must receive the ball before scoring in a box
2. Must receive when driving into the box

Match Play: Conditions: Demonstrate these before match play, reinforce throughout the match

1. Single hand release
2. CPA-One over, staggered start
3. BL-WD holding top/ball side

Cool down/Feedback: Question: What have we worked on today? What can we improve? What did we do well?

Movement

Aim: Understand the importance of driving forward and leading leg.

Warm up: Stuck in the mud.
Players run around in space with three players on, if you get tug by someone that is on you become stuck, stand with arms out, to be freed another player needs to run under your arm. Vary dynamic movement e.g. Lunge under arms and change which players are on.
Question: What type of movements do you do to get away from the player that is on?

Agility/Fitness: Each set 1minute

1. Forward drives: CPs, 'A' drives forward to receive from 'F' at pace, side steps back with an open body to ball, plants outside foot, accelerates and drives again, do not stop before catching the ball.
2. 'A' Sprints up and down the court whilst 'F' completes right hand shoulder pass against the wall.
3. 'F' becomes 'A' repeats the above.
4. Overs: CPs, 'A' sprints forward taps the ball in 'F's' hands opens the hips out travels back open to ball and receives an over, lands on the closest foot to 'F' passes the ball back and repeats but opens out the opposite side. 'F' needs to release the ball quickly and to the open space using single hand pass.
5. 'A' Sprints, 'F' completes left hand shoulder pass against the wall.
6. 'F' becomes 'A' repeats the above.
7. 45* with outward turn: CPs, 'A' drives out towards the right receives the ball in front, lands on right leg to turn out, fully turns (hips come through) before passing back to 'F' with left hand, then drives left landing on left leg, fully turns before passing back to 'F' with right hand. Ensure still driving forward not flat and turning out, 'F' ball placement in front.
8. 'A' Sprints, 'F' completes chest to over-head passes against the wall.
9. 'F' becomes 'A' repeats the above.

①   F→←‑A

②   F⇄‑‑A

③   F‑A

Drill 1: Leading leg to beat defender with no step back
'A' sets up on a court line with a cone acting as 'D' starts static and drives over the line when coach blows the whistle, repeats 6x each side. Repeats 6x each side starting from a fast feet position: CPs, no step back before going forward, lead with closest leg to 'D'.

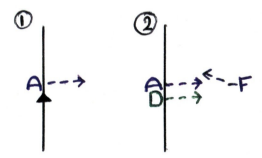

Progression: Replace cone for a player 'D', add a 'F' to release the ball to 'A', 'D' starts static then progresses to try and intercept the ball. CPs, 'A' needs to be definite and fast whilst 'F' needs to pass ahead in the space away from 'D'.

Drill 2: Think Tank, Change of direction-forward drive. 'A's drive out to receive from 'F's, must be a forward drive. 'A' passes back, drives back through the cones, changes direction and goes to another 'F'. Work for 1min then change roles, repeat twice. CPs, Timing, Vision, Speed, Ball placement

Progression:
'A' start with the ball and pass out to 'F', 'A' then drive forward to re receive their own ball, they then turn and pass to a different 'F' then drive through the circle change direction and re drive for own ball. CPs, Communication, Vision, Timing, Speed, Ball placement.

Drill 3: 2v1 'A' works for 20 consecutive passes in a box just under half a third in size, 'F's can move around the outside.
CPs, Definite movement from 'A', decision making from 'F'

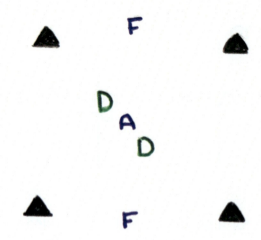

Conditioned game: 5 before goal

'A1' + 'A2' offer to 'F1'. 'F1' chooses who to pass to. If 'A1' gets the first ball, 'A2' must work for 2nd ball on circle edge, then delivers to 'A3' who off loads to 'A4'. 'A4' then sends the ball to 'F2' and they go again. Work for a set of 5, 'A3' shoots on the last one, everyone changes roles.

CPs, Definite drives, Timing, Ball placement, Communication

Question players: What type of movement do you use?

Progression:

1. Add in defence
2. Add in more passing conditions, e.g. one pass on circle edge
3. A3 can shoot each time they receive

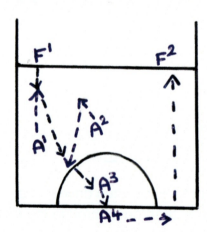

Match play: Conditions

1. Must drive forward to receive
2. Any errors that player runs a lap of the court

Cool down/Feedback: Question: What did we learn today? What could we improve on? What went well?

Samantha Griffin

Footwork

Aim: All players to understand and apply footwork rule.

Warm up: Sticky + steppy (sticky= landing foot, steppy= moving foot).

Juniors: Explain and demonstrate sticky + steppy.

All players in one third moving around, when coach blows whistle once, players land 2 feet, choose which foot is steppy- pivots then runs again. When coach blows whistle twice, players land 1,2, pivot and run again. Change the dynamic movement throughout.

Senior: Scatter spots around the court, players moving around on each spot they choose whether to land 2 footed or 1, pivot change direction and run to another. Add in a ball, players must receive near a spot.

Agility/fitness: 'A' sprint forwards, pushes off on the outside foot to get power. Sidestep across, ensure hips are facing forwards, push off and sprint forward. Repeat 3x, change sides.

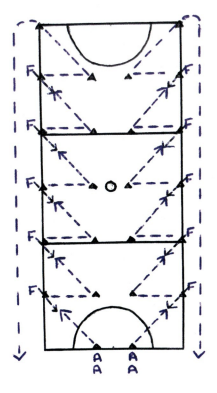

Progression:

Add 'F' so 'A' receives a ball on the forward drive. Work for 3x then change roles
CPs, Pushing off on outside foot, Hips facing direction in which moving, Speed, Ball placement

Drill: 'A' works in a box, coach calls numbers, 'A' must hit that number of cones before driving forward to receive from 'F'. Repeat x5 and change roles.
CPs, Outside foot, Open body angle, Driving forward

Progression:

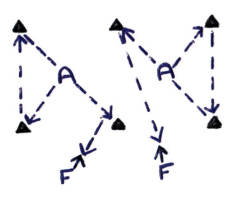

1. 2 boxes are now linked. 'A's' must communicate and change boxes, cannot have 2 'A's' in one box. CPs, Communication, Timing, Body angle, Outside foot
2. Add a defender, 2v1
3. 2v2

Seniors: Attacking team have to land on circle edge with the ball then play back to WD. GS also has to make a decision and come out to receive ball out at least once, whilst GA has to receive ball twice in circle. They have 4 attempts to complete the conditions and then play to goal.

CPs, Patience, Re-offer, Hitting circle edge, Ball placement

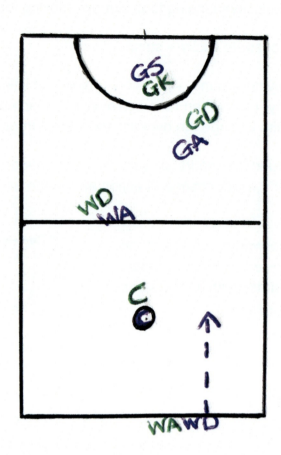

Match play

Cool down/Feedback: Question group, get them to discuss in pairs and then feedback

Samantha Griffin

Feeding a holding and moving player

Aim: Vision to feed a first-time ball.

Warm up: Coach leads a match day warm up. Fab Five, Dynamic movement, Paired ball work, Unit work, Game

Agility/Fitness: Anywhere ladder 1-10, 10-1. 'A' set up on the goal line with 'F' in front, receive one anywhere then sprint to halfway, return two anywheres then sprint, continue all the way to 10 and back down sprinting between every anywhere set. CPs, 'A' maintains basics, catching with two hands and strong passes back, 'F' vision and reaction to send the ball to space.

Drill 1: Feeding a holding player. In 3's, attacker holds from different angle, feeder makes 5x feeds to each angle. Defender starts passive.
CPs, technique for 'A' T up in the middle of 'D's back when holding behind, when in front stand strong and step onto the ball, strength using body. Technique for 'D' keep feet moving, change position. 'A' re-adjust feet as 'D' moves.
'F' adds touch the ball, sight 'D' space and 'A's body angle before releasing.

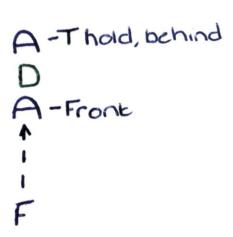

Progression:

1. Defender becomes active

Question: Why will 'F' change type of pass? Why is learning to hold beneficial to all?

Drill 2: Feeding long distance and to a moving player.
Players set up like a centre pass 'A2' drives out and receives from 'A1' then turns to pass to 'A3' who is static. 'A3' passes to 'A4' who has stepped up to centre circle whilst 'A1' and 'A2' move down one role and 'A3' comes to the side, repeat x10.
CPs, Strong accurate passes into space using single hand, A2 reaction over the line, turn out and fully before passing.

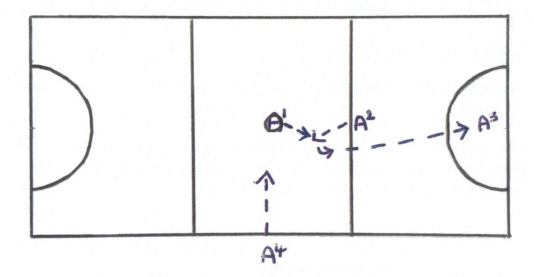

Progression:

1. 'A3' moves for ball, drives out and back to post, can shoot
2. Add defenders on to each 'A', 'A1' can become active and hit circle edge

Question: How many passes did it take to get to goal? Where should your vision be first?

Conditioned game: Possession/Melting pot
'A' must keep the ball, every 5 passes a 'D' enters.
If 'D' win ball or force errors teams change roles.
Conditions: 'A' must drive forward, ball above the head, 'A' clear and touch a line after each pass.
Have a couple of attempts then allow teams to discuss, then re-start.

Question: Why is keeping possession so important?

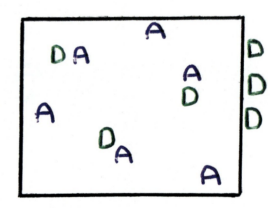

Match play: Conditions

1. Ball above the head
2. Must keep possession until reaches shooting opportunity- 5 star jumps for error

Cool down/Feedback: Question what did we learn today? Did we apply it to the court?

Samantha Griffin

Timing and Attacking Strategies

Aim: To be able to time movement successfully.

Warm up: Random dynamic movements with clear changes direction and changes in speed. Add a ball.

Agility/ fitness: M runs

'A1' sprints to third corner, changes direction to sprint to top of the circle edge, receive a pass to pass back, then return to opposite queue. 'A2' starts once 'A1' hits third line. Complete in ladder sets- x6, x3, x1 (1=when you are back to your original queue). Change feeder each set (rest).

CPs, Speed, Change of direction, Ball placement

Question: Why do players drive to circle edge?

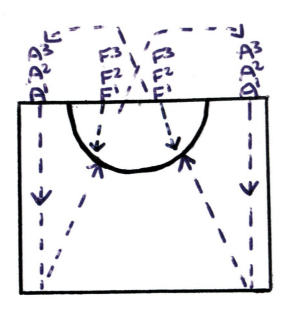

Drill 1: Timing, Attacker has to time drive. 'F' starts facing away from 'A' throws to themselves or against a wall, turns then passes to 'A' who is driving forward to the ball, x6 change.

Question: How do we know when the feeder is ready to throw? (CPs, Eye contact, Balanced body position)

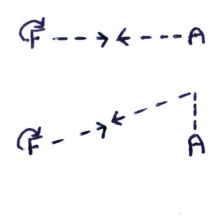

Progression 1: Add prelim move

Question: What is a prelim move? (dodge/change of direction)

'A' now must complete prelim move before driving forward- ensuring they time correctly, x6 change.

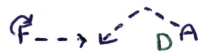

Progression 2: Add a defender

Drill 2: Double feed drill, 2x 'F's' both with a ball. 'A' offers to 'F1' receives and returns the ball then offers from 'F2'. Change 'F's' every 5 attackers. 'A' needs to think about the movement between feeders.

Progression:

1. Attackers increase to 3 offers
2. Add a defender

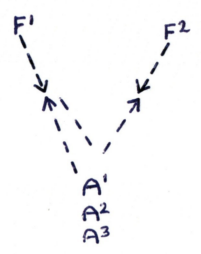

Conditioned game: Drive or Sprint
Teams try to make 20 passes without losing possession, if they do, they must sprint to their line before returning to the third. Condition: players must drive forward

Progression

1. Add another team

Samantha Griffin

Question: Why do we want to keep possession? (to win)
Why in this game is keeping possession hard? (fatigue)
What does this prepare you for? (matches, last quarter, tournaments)

Match play

Cool down/Feedback: Question: What have we developed? What did we do well?

Creating space

Aim: Understand when to create space for yourself or another player.

Warm up: All players in the goal circle completing dynamic movement. Extend space to the goal third, then into full court, then restrict back down. CPs, Vision
Repeat with players in pairs passing a ball

Question: Why were you unable to warm up properly in the goal circle?
As the space increased what did you find?
What did you find when you repeated with a ball?

Fitness/agility: Players in pairs, passing ladder

Make 2 passes, sprint for 1 (goal line and back = 1)

Make 4 passes, sprint for 2 (1 player runs with the ball)

Make 6 passes, sprint for 3

Make 8 passes, sprint for 4

Make 10 passes, sprint for 5

Then work back down.

CPs, Accuracy, Speed

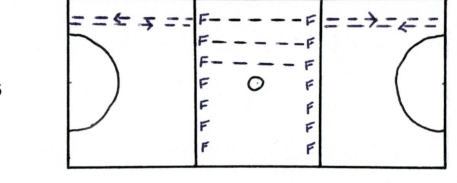

Drill: 3 Man Weave
Players use 3 channels on court to pass and move the ball down the court, driving to gain depth. Three players start at the top of the court in line, spaced in 3 channels. The ball starts with the middle player in front of the post. The other two players start to move down the court, the player with the ball can choose who they pass to. The moving player that does not receive the ball must then change to the middle channel whilst continuing to gain depth, whilst the player that just threw the ball moves into the empty wide channel. Continue all the way through the court with the ball always being thrown to the free player moving into the empty channel.

Progression

1. Add a cut back and forward drive
2. Add defenders

CPs, Speed, Depth, Accurate passing, Landing balanced

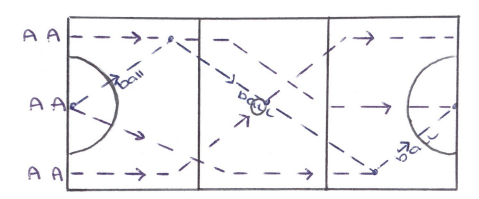

Conditioned game: Through court play

1. Everyone should receive the ball
2. Always 2 options for each ball
3. Players support- back up
4. Repeat 5x and have balls ready at end of court
5. Change new team on

CPs, Definite drives, Reading off, Vision, Single hand pass

Progression: Add defence

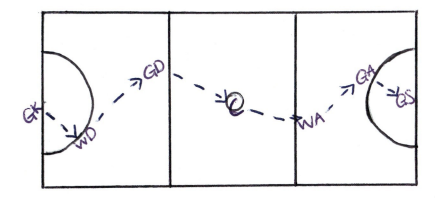

Match play:
Condition: ball cannot travel for 2 passes in a row in the same channel

Cool down/Feedback: Question, what did we learn today? What can we improve? What went well?

Attacking ball through court

Aim: To successfully attack the ball through the court as a team.

Warm up: Dynamic movement through the court. Tag rugby, score by putting the ball down at the goal line. If tug whilst in possession of the ball give to opposition team.

Agility: Circuit 1min at each station x3

1. Up and over cones, sidestep, forward drive, open body angle, receive high ball
2. Vary footwork through the ladder, 'F' can feed at any time
3. Fast feet between cones, hop to hold on outside leg, receive ball
4. Anywhere reaction, 'A' picks up ball and passes to 'F' without a ball, 'F' varies ball placement

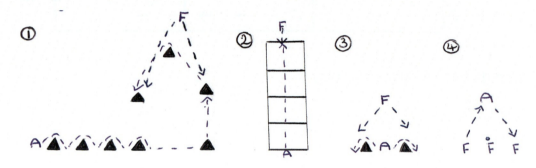

Drill 1: Attacking through court

Play ball through court x5, if working with a small group use the length, however if you have a large group, use the width.

Get players thinking about how they offer for the ball, create space for others, when they back up and where to. Ensure players are driving at speed, turning outwards, moving at the right time, and accurately passing the ball. Break down and talk about before repeating.

Progression:

1. Add defence

CPs, Timing, Forward drives, Speed, Quick release, Ball placement, Change in channel

Samantha Griffin

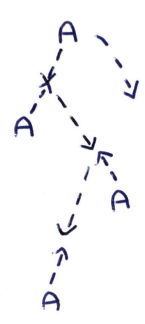

Transition: Split into half court. Two teams in each half. 'A' aim to get the ball from one end to the other to get 1 point. Keep attacking ball unless defence turn over. On coach's whistle, ball down and 'D' becomes 'A'

CPs, Communication, Speed, Reaction, Vision

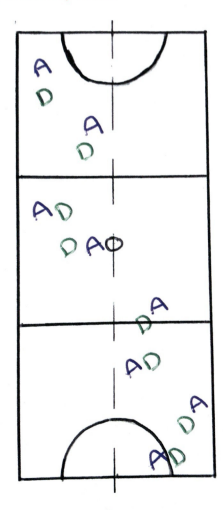

Match play:

1. Continue to break down any errors
2. Check for staggered start on c's
3. Check backline set ups

Cool down/Feedback: Split players into pairs to debrief the session.
Question: What did we work on today?
What went well?
What did you find challenging?

Options

Aim: Understand the three options that need to be provided for every ball.

Warm up: Player led; dynamic movement followed by game.

Options: Complete 20 successful of each set

1. Lateral - forward   2. 2nd forward   3. 2nd forward - diagonal   4. Cut back

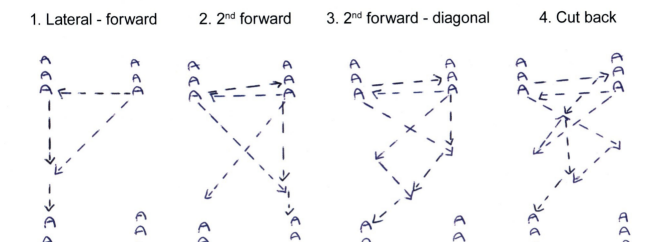

In drill one once you have passed the forward change to the queue parallel to you. Once you have worked to receive the forward join the opposite queue. Keep queues balanced.

Progression:

1. Add 2 defenders, attackers then need to make the correct decision on the options they provide and adapt to the defence.

CPs, Commitment to drive, Speed, Ball placement, Vision, Communication

Conditioned game:
Start ball at GS. Closest 'A' offers first then turns and passes to the next 'A' the ball works through all 3 'A's who are only aloud in 1 third until it reaches the next GS who shoots. Aim attack the ball through the middle channel. 'A's move to the next box once passed the ball.

Progression:

1. Add defence
2. 'A' can move 1 third ahead than the one they started in
3. 'A' can pass to the 'A' waiting in the box

CPs, Commitment to drive, Speed, Ball placement, Vision, Communication, Options, Decision
Forward + back movement + jump squats making

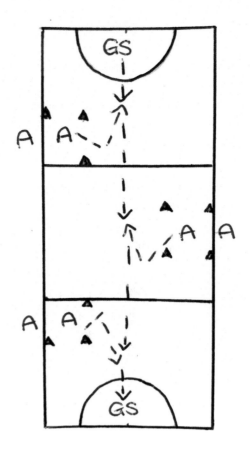

Match play

Cool down/Feedback: Question what are the three types of options?

Defence

Key: Dictate as a unit

Stage 1 Defence Ball Side

Aim: To develop skills to man mark (stage 1) ball side.

Warm Up: 'Tails'. All players have a bib tucked in the top of their shorts, majority of the bib must be hanging down, try to steal each other's, player with the most bibs or still with tail wins. Repeat 3x.

Question: What types of movement do you do to protect your bib?

Fitness/ Agility: Forward + back movement + jump squats
Players move forward then back at pace thinking about body angle, should cover the length of a third complete 4x forward + back 1, then complete 10 jump squats = 1 set. Repeat for 3 sets.

Drill 1: Shadowing
'A' can move anywhere in the square
CPs, Vision, Awareness, footwork
Question: What do you need to do to stay with 'A

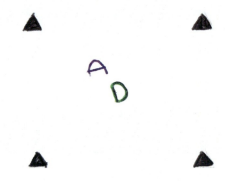

Drill 2: Marking the Player (Ball side)
'A' works at 25% trying to get ball from 'F' making sure to reset to middle each time. 'D' works for 6 intercepts, then changes roles.
CPs, Body balanced, start halfway across 'A's body, head up, open body angle to ball and 'A', run feet when going for the ball.
Progression: 'A' increases intensity

Samantha Griffin

Conditioned Game: 3v3

3D V 3A in half a third. Attack need to make 10 consecutive passes. Defence get 1 point for every intercept. After 1 minute of work feedback score and then as unit, repeat implementing feedback. Change roles.

CPs, Apply pressure all man to man.

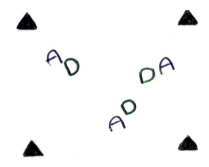

Match Play: Focus on every player man marking

Cool down/Feedback

Dictating High and Wide

Aim: To develop and apply skills to dictate high and wide (Man to man defence, goal side)

Warm up: Dynamic movement through court. Rats and Rabbits, players stand in the middle third in two lines opposite each other, name the lines Rats, Rabbits. When coach calls Rats, they aim to get to their closest side-line before the Rabbits tig them. If coach calls Rabbits, they aim to get to their closest side-line before the Rats tig them. Each time teams must reset quickly; coach can call at any point.

Agility: Developing balance and footwork

1 min – skipping

1 min – single leg hold (left)

1 min – skipping

1 min – single leg hold (right)

1 min – skipping

Drill 1: Restricting the attacker
'A' tries to touch as many cones as possible but cannot go to the same cone twice in a row.
'D' using body angle, must dictate 'A' to one cone or out of the box.
Work for 1 minute then change, repeat x2.
CPs, Dictate, Body on Body, Strength, Narrow base

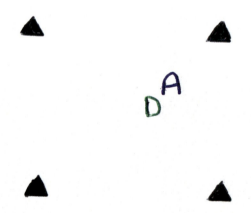

Drill 2: Dictating high and wide
'A' working to receive the ball on the cones.
'D' starts goal side dictating 'A' high + wide. If 'A' gets behind, 'D' transitions to ball side.
Work for 1 minute then change

Samantha Griffin

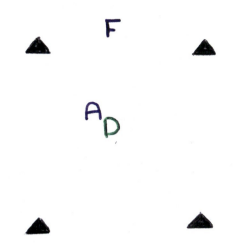

Drill 3: Recovering to ball side

'A' starts with the ball and passes to 'F'. 'A' must work herself and the ball over the line.

'D' needs to keep 'A' high for 3 seconds, if not force wide away from ball so can defend from a ball side position and aim to intercept.

Work until 'D' forces 4 errors or interceptions.

CPs, Body Angle, Vision, Strength

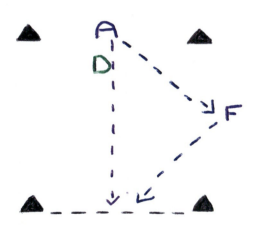

Conditioned Game:

Court is broken into two sides. 'A1', 'A2', 'D1', 'D2' only allowed on one side, 'A3', 'D3' only allowed in the circle.

'A4's not allowed into attacking third.

Attackers aim to get the ball to circle edge before feeding to 'A3'.

Defence must dictate high + wide to keep 'A' from getting to circle edge. Ball can be passed between the two sides.

Play through 6x before changing roles.
Complete with attackers defending a back line.

Progression:

1. Add 'D4'
2. Court restrictions removed

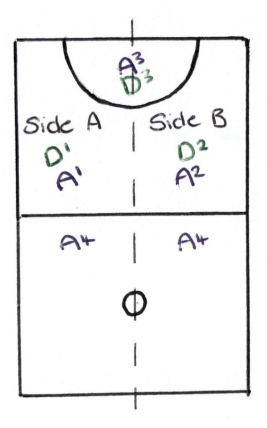

Match Play:
Conditions are all players must attempt to dictate their opposing player to keep them high and wide. Count how many errors the defence force.

Cool down/Feedback

Samantha Griffin

Dictating on and off the body

Aim: Dictating on and off the body

Warm up: Bousers Castle
Create a larger circle around the centre circle and fill with cones = 1 point, 6 bibs = 3 points, 1 tennis ball = 5 points. Split the group into as many teams as you want. One team defends the castle (area with objects) they cannot enter the area so need to tig attackers before. Attacking teams given a base on the outside of the court. Their aim is to get into the castle and collect an object. Can only collect one object at a time if tug on the way must go back to their base before going again. Play for 2 mins then change the team's roles so that everyone defends the castle. Give each team chance to talk between each attempt to try and come up with a strategy. Collect scores each time, the team that had the least points taken off them when defending wins.

Agility/Fitness: Split into teams, set up a line of 4 cones for each team with a ball, placed in line with the centre circle. Each cone has a number, coach calls numbers players must hit the numbers in order whilst going back to the line in-between each one. Once they have completed the number sequence, race to get the ball and hold above their head. Repeat until each player completes 4 attempts. Team with the most points at the end win and set a forfeit.

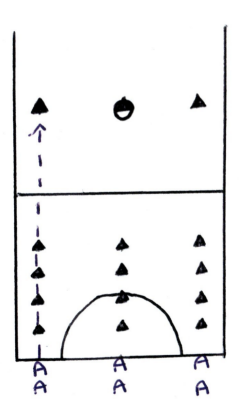

Drill 1: 'F' drops the ball in, the first player to get the ball becomes the attacker, 'A's aim is to work for 10 points.

Receiving any ball = 1 point

Crossing the line to receive = 2 points

Receiving in the back space = 3 points

'D' aims to dictate to restrict 'A's space and to win the ball, force error. Change the 'F', everyone needs to complete each role 3x. Feedback to each other in-between sets.

CPs, Body angle, Narrow base, Vision, Timing

F
← line to cross

A D

Back space

Drill 2: 'D' limit 'A1' from getting the ball, time coming off to intercept pass to 'A2' who starts static. Work until 'D' intercepts 3, change roles

Progression: 'A2' drives down court

CPs, Body angle, Narrow base, Vision, Timing

F   A²
ball   (2nd part)

A¹   D   A²

Conditioned Game: WA & C work to make 8 passes in the box, can use GS on the outside, if they make 8, they can continue to attack to goal. GD, WD aim to intercept the ball, they must off load to GK first and then continue to attack the ball to goal. First team to score 3 wins then change over which team starts off defending.

CPs, Communication, Decision making, Timing

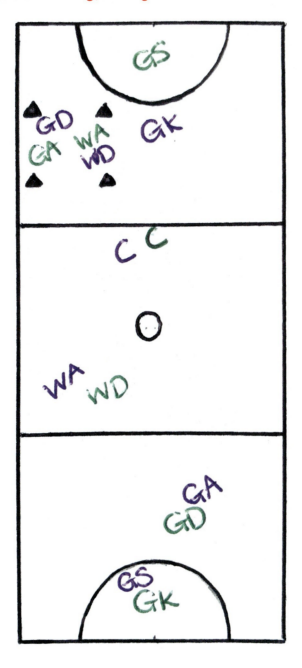

Match Play: Give points for team that scores following on from a turnover

Cool down/Feedback

Marking the Ball (2nd Stage)

Aim: To understand how to apply pressure to the player with the ball. Be able to apply this without causing obstruction.

Warm up: Give half of the group a ball, players can move with the ball and pass at any point. Keep changing the type of dynamic movement throughout. When the coach blows the whistle players with the ball must stand still, whilst those without react to set up a 3ft mark on a player with the ball. Restart the movement after 3 seconds.

Discuss any challenges of setting up a 3ft mark? What are you trying to achieve by marking the ball?

Agility/Fitness: In pairs players work on jumping and balance. 1 minute on each exercise repeat the set twice.

Jump taps: start by holding the ball tall above your head against the wall, mark where you can reach. Jump up and tap the ball as high as you can, see how far above your mark you can get, land soft and then repeat for 1 minute trying to remain consistent with how high you can jump. Both players to work at the same time.

Balance & Reach: start by standing on your right leg, players pass to each other varying the direction of the ball to see how far they can stretch out remaining balanced, if you take the ball with one hand bring it back to two before passing.

Repeat jump taps then back to Balance & Reach on your left leg = 1 complete set.

Drill 1: 3ft Mark

In 3's, two attackers, one defender. Attackers must hold the ball for 3 seconds. 'D' needs to set up 3ft away from 'As' landing foot, 'A' moves the ball left to right hand and chest to over release points. 'D' needs to keep pressuring the ball even when 'A' changes her release. 'D' needs to stretch as much as they can to pressure the ball remaining balanced on 2 feet, on the third second try and jump to tip the ball. 'D' then recovers to mark the second 'A'. Repeat x 6 change roles.

Progression:

1. 'D' stays lower with arms and times the jump to intercept the pass.
2. 'A' can release at any point

Samantha Griffin

CPs, Balance, Vision, Timing, Recovery

Drill 2: Recovery
In pairs, set up Infront of a wall with 'A' facing ready to pass against it. 'D' starts by marking the ball aiming to pressure the pass or tip to intercept. If the ball gets passed 'D', 'D' needs to react turning to box out 'A' to catch the ball before them. Repeat x 6 change roles.

Question: Which positions will box out most in a game? When? Why?
CPs, Balance, Vison, Timing, Recovery, Narrow base, Fast feet

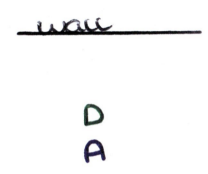

Drill 3: 5ft mark, engaging with another player (Near Side)
'A' works to receive the ball. If successful resets to the middle of the box.

'D1' dictates 'A' towards the ball to connect with 'D2', 'D2' is in a 5ft mark. 'D1' needs to communicate with 'D2' to intercept the ball. 'D2' needs to open out their body slightly to the direction in which they are called so they can sight the 'A' and the ball. Work until defence intercept 6. Use a line to help the 'D' see if they have dictated 'A' the correct side to the ball.

CPs, Balance, Vison, Timing, Recovery, Narrow base, Fast feet, Body angle

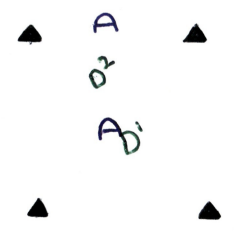

Conditioned Game: Unit defence

'D1' works on 5 ft mark opening body angle to intercept. 'D2', 'D3' dictate and communicate. Work for 6 intercepts/errors then change. Attackers can switch sides and continue to move in the space. Defence need to work together to force the error e.g. both dictate the same side or one near, one far.

CPs, Communication, Vison, Footwork, Body angle

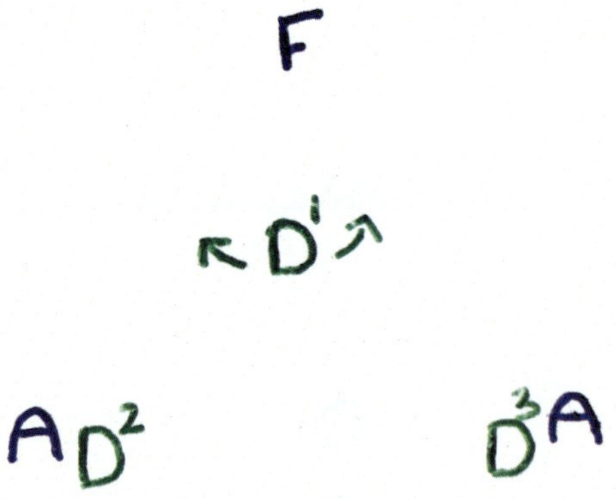

F

↖ D¹ ↗

A D²   D³ A

Match Play: Condition all players must attempt a 3ft or 5ft mark when their opposing player has the ball. At half time question what happened when players applied defensive pressure to the ball.

Cool down/Feedback

Question: Why do we want to apply pressure to the ball? How can we do this?

Samantha Griffin

Near Side/Far Side Defence

Aim: To understand Near Side is to dictate towards the ball and engage with another defender and Far Side is to dictate away from the ball.

Warm up: Everyone in one court moving around at a slow jog, changing direction with head up.

Whistle 1= faster jog

Whistle 2= sprint (must be clear change of pace)

Then whistle 1 to slow down. Work for 2-3 minutes

Agility/ Fitness: Sprint work, in 2 lines in centre third, number these lines. Put 12 balls along the top wall.

Instructions to shout:
1 = 1's sprint to their side-line and back
2 = 2's sprint to their side-line and back
3 = 2's trying to catch 1's
4 = 1's trying to catch 2's
Complete for 1 minute then add:
5 = Sprint to a ball and complete 10 chest passes, or sprint length of court if did not get ball
6 = sprint to your side-line then ball (same as above)

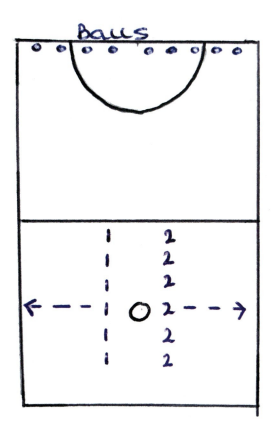

Drills 1: Near Side

'A' works to receive the ball. If successful resets (set spots up as a line).

'D1' dictates 'A' towards the ball to connect with 'D2', 'D2' is in a 5ft mark. 'D1' needs to communicate with 'D2' to intercept the ball. Work until defence intercept 6. Use a line to help the 'D' see if they have dictated 'A' the correct side to the ball.

CPs, Body angle, Vision, Strength, Footwork, Communication

Drill 2: Far Side

'A' works to receive the ball. If successful resets (set spots up as a line). 'D1' dictates 'A' away from the ball, can communicate 'D2' to change angle, 'D1' aim to run feet and take the intercept. Work until defence intercept 6.

CPs, Body angle, Vision, Strength, Footwork, Communication

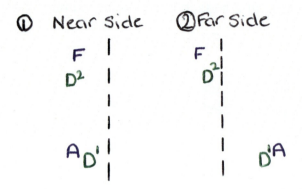

Question: What is near side defence? (Dictating towards the ball to engage with another 'D') What is far side defence? (Dictating away from the ball)

Drill 3: Unit defence

'D1' works on 5 ft mark opening body angle to intercept. 'D2', 'D3' dictate and communicate. Work for 6 intercepts/errors then change. Attackers can switch sides and continue to move in the space. Defence need to work together to force the error e.g. both dictate the same side or one near one far.

CPs, Communication, Vison, Footwork, Body angle

Samantha Griffin

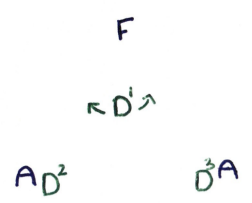

Conditioned Games: 2v2

'A's trying to work the ball from third line to goal line and back to get a point.

6 attempts then change roles. 'D' aiming to dictate and work together to gain turn over.

CPs, Dictate, Strength, Communication

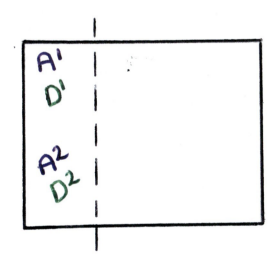

Match Play: Aim is for players to react to the situation to set up Near Side/Far Side. Pause game to check and challenge.

Cool down/Feedback:

Question:

1. What styles of defence are we learning?
2. What is near side?
3. What is far side?
4. What skills do we need to be a good defender?

Intercepting

Aim: Learn how to successfully intercept.

Warm up: Traffic light. Each third has a colour, Green, Amber, Red. Players start within the centre third (Amber), coach calls colours players race to those colours. Start with it not being a race and changing the dynamic movement. Then finish with it being competitive, last player to the colour is out.

Agility: Set 4 cones up in a straight line running parallel, around 3m off a court line e.g. third line/goal line. Each player has a set of cones and a ball. Number the cones 1-4, player starts on 1 and throws the ball to 4, must then run after the ball in a straight line and catch before a 2nd bounce. Progress to adding a change, player starts on 2 throws to 4 must run to 1 then to 4. Ensure you start from both sides to change which foot the player changes direction on.

Progression:

1. Players start on the court line, coach calls numbers they run forward to that number and then back to the line keeping their body angle open to their cones.
2. Add the ball, player starts on the line then throws the ball to a cone, once it has bounced they can chase and try and receive before a second bounce

CPs, Quick feet, Body angle, Vision

Drill 1: Figure of 8
'F's pass the ball at a steady consistent pace.
'D' starts behind and times coming around 'F' to take the ball with 2 hands. Then offloads the ball to 'F' and recovers to next 'F' before repeating.
Work for 10, aim to get every pass (quick recovery).
CPs, Body Angle, Getting feet around, Leading with inside arm and leg to avoid contact, Hands to ball, Speed, Vision

Drill 2: Piggy in the middle
'F's pass the ball in a set order at chest height. 'D' working to intercept 6x before changing roles.
'D' needs to think about recovery and set up, do not chase the ball.

Progression:

Samantha Griffin

1. Ball can be passed in any order
2. Height of ball varied
3. Triangle made bigger

CPs, Body Angle, Getting feet around, Hands to ball, Speed, Vision

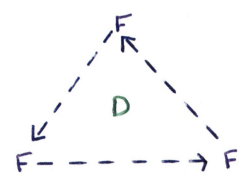

Drill 3: Reading the pass

'F's pass the ball either between themselves or can pass to 'A's. If 'A' receives from 'F1' she must pass to 'F2'.

'D' needs to do job of tracking 'A' ball side to stop them getting the ball but also time intercept.

Have confidence to win ball. If it is too hard move 'A's in closer.

Make 4 intercepts each before changing roles.

CPs, Body Angle, Getting feet around, Hands to ball, Speed, Vision, Communication

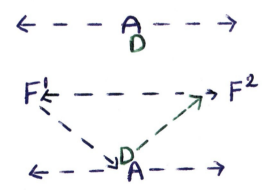

Conditioned Game 1:

Split third up as shown. 'D's only allowed in 1 area. 'A's can change but there can never be two in the same box. 'A's aim to make 15 passes. 'D's aim to stop them by forcing error or intercepting. Change roles after defence gain 3 intercepts.

Progression:

1. 'D' can change boxes but never two in one box.

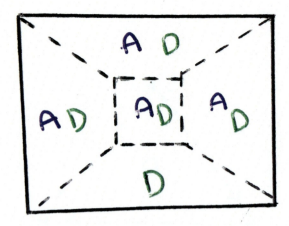

Conditioned Game 2: Time trial
Team works to keep the ball for 1 minute. The team that ends up without the ball at the end runs suicides. Should promote 'D' making interceptions then keeping the ball.
Change which team starts with the ball each time.

CP's, communication, working as a unit

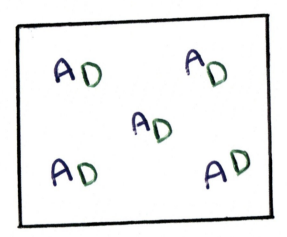

Match Play: Give points for interceptions.

Cool Down/Feedback

Samantha Griffin

Unit Defence

Aim: Working as a unit

Warm Up: Ball Tag
Two even teams working in centre third. One team starts with ball and must get all the other team out by tagging them with the ball, netball rules apply. One attempt each.

Agility/Fitness: Team Anywheres
'W' works for 3 anywhere balls from each feeder, them completes 1 suicide, making sure they get back to feed for next worker.

CPs, quick feet, 2 hands on ball

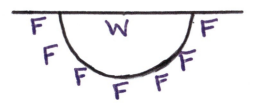

Drill 1: Communication as a pair
'F's can move around the box and pass to each other. Both 'F's feeding ball into space for 'D's to react and pick up.
'D's need to communicate so that always one covering left and right, front and back.
Work for 10 balls then change roles. Circle defenders can do this drill in the circle

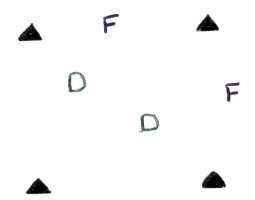

Progression:

1. One 'F' can attempt to walk (speed up) through box. One 'D' has to stop 'F' getting to other side, whilst other 'D' picking up the ball.
2. Add an attacker into the box working to receive the ball, 'D' needs to stop this, whilst reacting to any loose balls.

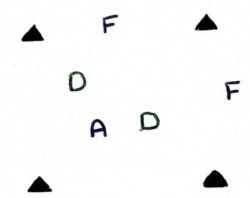

Drill 2: Variety of Marking the Shot/Pass
Circle defence, work together to lean, jump shot, boxing out against shooters
Mid court work in groups of 3's. Two players passing the ball with one defending the pass, practicing stage 2 defence arms over. Apply as much pressure to the ball as possible, try jumping on 3 seconds to intercept.

CPs, Ensure 3ft from attackers landing food, Balance, Timing, Vision

Conditioned Game: Smart Possession

Circle 'D' set up in circle

Centre court in centre third

Attack working to make 20 passes = 1 point. 3 attackers start on the outside, inside attack can pass out but once they have, they follow the ball out to become an outside attacker, whilst the outside attacker moves in once they have released the ball.

'D' working together to intercept. 'D' thinks about high and wide, dictating, taking intercept. If 'D' intercept or force the error, they become the attacking team. First to 3 points wins.

CPs, Communication, Strength, must all do your job

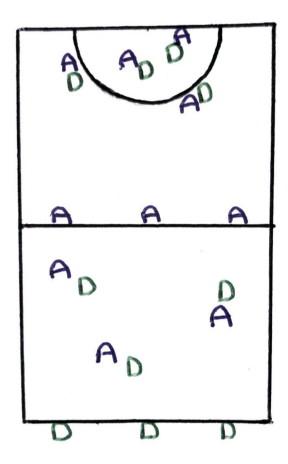

Match Play: Two points if the goal is scored from a turnover

Cool Down/Feedback

Transition

Aim: To be able to make quick and successful decisions when transitioning.

Warm up: In pairs, both players with a ball. One player leads a movement in space with the ball moving, whilst other player copy's that movement and follows the player, when coach blows the whistle the role is reversed.

Agility: In 2s compete for ball

1. Standing
2. Facing away
3. Sitting down
4. Lying down

Conditioned Game 1: 3 Defenders
'A's work for 10 passes can use 'F', can switch channels but never catch the ball with another 'A' in the same channel.
'D's are restricted to one channel each, need to work together to intercept or force error. Change defence once 3 sets of 'As' have worked.

Progression:
1.Add a 3rd attacker
CPs, Communication, Strength, Dictate

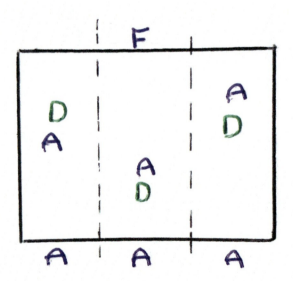

Conditioned Game 2: Transitioning
Purple 'A' aims to attack ball to line to receive one point. If 'D' intercept, then they attack opposite way. Whoever scores come straight off court and Red 'A' start to attack. First to 5 points.
CPs, Transition, reaction, communication, body angles

Samantha Griffin

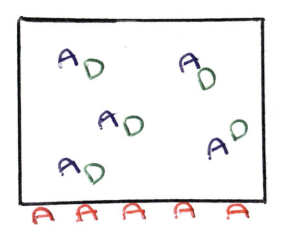

Conditioned Game 3: Transitioning positional

Attacking positions attack to goal, Defensive positions halfway (in line with C circle)

'A' transition to defending when 'D' gets the rebound. New 'A' in when 'D' passes the ball off.

New 'D' in on rebound from a goal.

Play for 5mins, talk in teams, repeat

CPs, Communication, Reaction, Vision, Placement

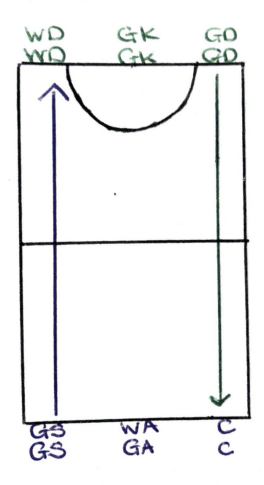

Match Play:

Take stats on turn overs to goal. Discuss the successes and what they could do better.

Cool down/Feedback

Strategies
Part 1

Restart Session

Aim: Raise intensity recap basic principles.

Warm up: Player led

1. Activation
2. Dynamic
3. Speed
4. Ball

Agility: Netball Circuit, 1 minute at each station

1. 'A'. drives forward to the top cone, sidesteps back diagonally, forward, back, drive forward for ball, change roles with 'F'. Keep body angle open to the ball, push off on outside foot.
2. Up and oversteps, sidesteps, drive forward, receive ball, pass, back, 'F' drops ball 'A' picks up and becomes 'F'.
3. 'D' completes figure of 8 around the cones, drives out to the left cone receives, then drives across to receive, 'F' pass ahead stretching 'D' as if taking an intercept. 'F' drops the ball 'D' picks up, change roles.
4. 'D1' and 'D2' start behind different 'F' drive around creating figure of 8, receive the ball then pass back. Keeping body angle open and accelerating as they come by 'F'. Change roles after 10 balls.
5. 2v2 'A' work to make 10 passes if 'D' intercept the9y become 'A'.
6. 'A' drive forward receive a ball, pass back, run forward to receive a drop ball, pass back, drive across to receive a ball, pass back, turn the hips driving away from 'F' to receive an over, change roles.

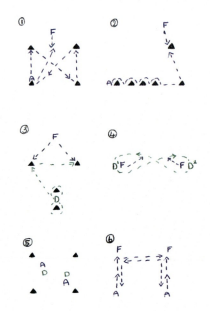

CPs, Strong Drives, Body Angles, Footwork, Accurate passing.

Samantha Griffin

Conditioned Game: Through the boxes

Attack must work the ball through court to goal, ball must be received in box 1, 2, 3 before it can go to goal. Only one attacker in a box, no defence.

Ball starts with player on the goal line. Team transition to shoot other way.

Aim to get 3 consecutive goals.

If 'D' let 3 go – sprint for 3

If 'A' only gets 1 sprint for 2

CPs, Communication, Timing, Vision, Definite movements

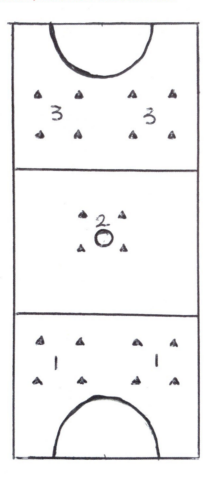

In 2 teams recap attack and defence so far

Question: What are the attacking and defensive principles we have covered? What is our aim when attacking and defending?

Match Play:

Conditions:

1. 3 seconds before throwing
2. Run on error
3. Keep centre if you score

Cool down/Feedback

Centre Pass Attack Principles

Aim: Understand how to be available for the ball on CPA.

Warm up: Player led

1. Activation
2. Dynamic
3. Speed
4. Ball

Drill 1: 'Gate Tag'
2x gates.
'D' starts in the middle.
'A' aim to get through one of the gates without getting tug
6x each, change defender every 4
CPs, Definite movement, Speed, Change of direction, Vision

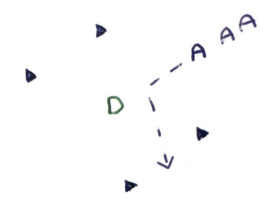

Drill 2: 1st phase (getting over the line)
'A1' acts as centre, feeds to 'A2' then turns to 'A3' 6x each side change roles.
CPs:
'A1' Ball placement, decision making
'A2' Speed, strength, timing
'A3', Prelim move, speed, commitment

Samantha Griffin

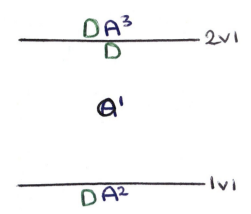

Drill 3: 2nd phase (gaining depth)

Attack work to attack the ball from one feeder to the next. Must decide who is going first, who is getting depth and react if it needs to change. There and back = 1 work for 6 then change roles.

CPs, Communication, speed, taking on a defender

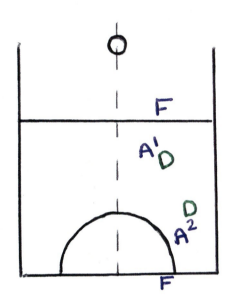

CPA set up:

1. Staggered start so players can read off, 1 on the line, 1 off the line. Aim for 1 player over the line at a time
2. If WA receives, GA get depth pull wide to open middle channel for C. GA aiming to be the forward option
3. C drives the middle channel
4. WD backs up on third line
5. Repeat x12 changing 1st phase and 2nd phase options

CPs, Communication, Reading off, Vision, Definite drives, Ball placement

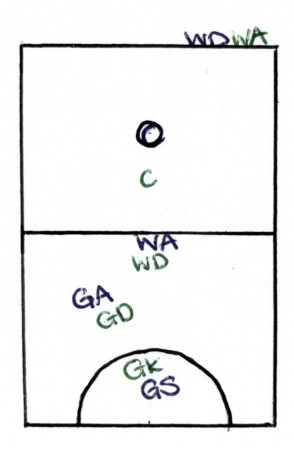

Match Play:

1. Set target of 5 consecutive centres
2. Take centre stats
3. Make corrections where needed

Cool down/Feedback

Samantha Griffin

Centre Pass Strategies

Aim: To be able to set up varied CPA strategies and work together as a unit.

Warm up: Player led

1. Activation
2. Dynamic
3. Speed
4. Ball

Agility: Reacting to the whistle
Start behind the line, on the whistle race to next line, x4 each
Add a cone as acting defender to practice leading with correct leg
CPs, Reaction, Speed, Leading leg closest to defender, No step back

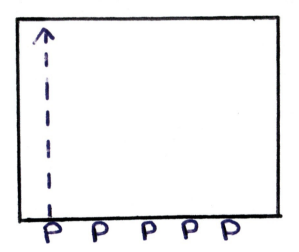

1st phase set ups:
Staggered: 1 on the line, one off
Read off each other, if option one does not work clear, allow second player to come through
C take middle on 2nd phase
CPs, Communication early, Definite drives, Ball placement, Vision, Body angle

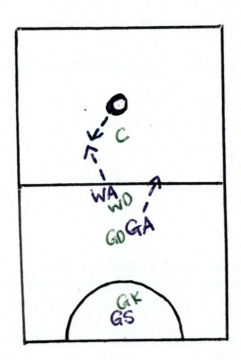

Screen

Either player can screen for the other and set up inside/outside.

Vision, if does not work player setting the screen comes off and drives forward.

2nd phase screening player tries to receive in the forward

CPs, Communication early, Definite drives, Ball placement, Vision. Body angle

Stack

Samantha Griffin

Stack for defender to receive, leading player on stack still offers
CPs, Communication early, Definite drives, Ball placement, Vision, Reading off

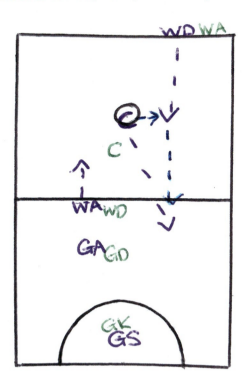

Zero Phase

Set up early to beat 'D' to the line.
Look at each other to allow a staggered drive
CPs, Communication early, Definite drives, Ball placement, Body angle, Vision

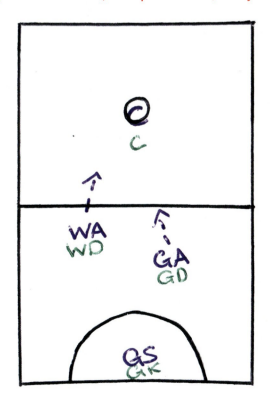

2nd Phase: No set rule, players aim is to get depth

Ball goes immediately, player cuts back resets to allow everyone time

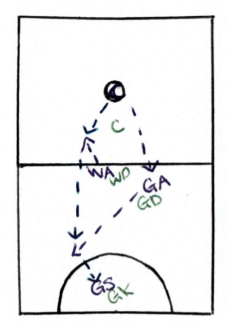 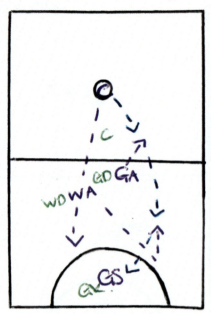 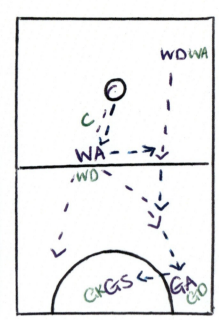

Play through each option 6x

CPs, Communication early, Definite drives, Ball placement, Speed

Conditioned Game:
Half court
6 attacking centres
6 backlines

Match Play: Count centre pass stats

Cool down/Feedback

Samantha Griffin

Defensive Backline

Aim: To be able to successfully play the ball from the defensive backline.

Warm up: Player led

1. Activation
2. Dynamic
3. Speed
4. Ball

Fitness/ Agility:
'A' completes figures of 8 around cones, on coaches' commands:

Forward, sprint to front cone + back

Back, sprint to back cone + back

Change figure of 8 to fast feet between cones to hops on the outer cones landing on outside foot, hold for a second.

Work for 40 seconds x6 1minute rest in between

CPs, body angle, control, footwork

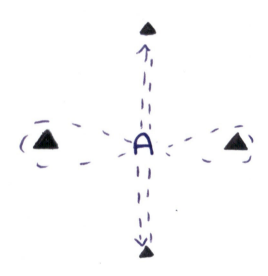

Drill: Backline options
Run through set ups no defence, practice passing to both options on each set up e.g. option 1 GK also passes to GD. Give the long ball x6

Progression:

1. Only give ball when player cuts forward
2. Add defence

CPs, 2 options, Decision making

Option 1: WD top Option 2: WD ball side Option 3: GD/WD open for C

Make Competitive: 2 teams have 6 attempts to complete a successful back line. Team that has highest success rate wins.

Match Play: No Centres after a goal take the ball from the GK.

Cool Down/Feedback

Centre Pass Defence

Aim: Setting up defensively on oppositions CPA

Warm up: Player led

1. Activation
2. Dynamic
3. Speed
4. Ball

Fitness/ Agility:

30 seconds – as many sprints as possible (keep score) add between each ball handling (below)

100 chest passes

30 seconds

100 overhead

30 seconds

100 right hand shoulder passes

30 seconds

100 left hand shoulder passes

30 seconds

100 right wall taps

30 seconds

100 left wall taps

30 seconds

Defensive Set ups:
1st phase wide, stopping depth on 2nd
- C marking the ball on an angle
- WD/GD straight out 1st phase and then play to recovery position on 2nd phase
- WA/GA flooding 1st phase
- C stay on ball to delay C run on 2nd phase

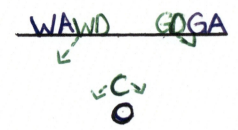

1st phase squeeze, stopping depth on 2nd

-WD/GD be strong and overload middle

- C to cover middle

- WA/GA work hard to dictate wide

CPs, Communication, Body angle, Footwork

2V1

- 2 on 1 does not receive the ball. Be aggressive over line and step into the space to dictate

- 1 on 1 zero phase keep from the line or force wide and contest. Angle inside and slightly behind to force high

- Slide behind 2nd phase to stop depth deny forward option

CPs, Communication, Body angle, Footwork

Samantha Griffin

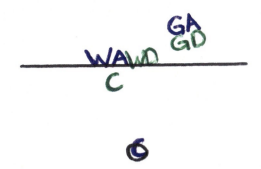

How can attack get involved?
-GS pick up a WD/GD so WA/GA can go 2v1 on either WD/GD
-Defensive end zero phase to put pressure on C to force the centre pass
CPs, Communication, Body angle, Footwork

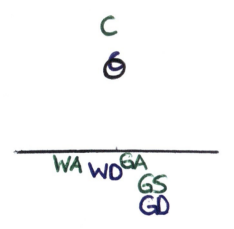

Match Play: Check for defensive set ups, focus team talks around them.

Cool down/Feedback

Circle rotation and hitting circle edge

Aim: To gain and understanding of Circle rotation and hitting circle edge

Warm up: Player led

1. Activation
2. Dynamic
3. Speed
4. Ball

Fitness/ Agility: Change of direct races
4 groups are competing against each other
Coach calls sequence of numbers, players race to hit cones in order and hold ball up when complete
First player to hold ball up wins 1 point

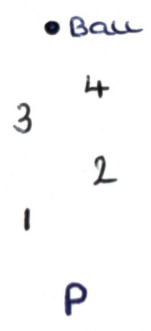

Circle Rotation:
Explain rotation, one front, one back, one left, one right. Pull the circle like a pendulum when one moves forward the other back and so on. Cutting the cake, always moving to and from the post (angles). Player at the back communicates.
Begin rotation with no ball in, ball can move around circle edge, so shooters body angles change always staying open to the ball and goal
CPs, Definite movement, Vision, Body angles, Speed

Samantha Griffin

Progression:

1. Work for 10x feeds then shoot (break play down where needed)
2. Add 1 defender
3. Add 2 defender

Rotation out of the circle:

Play through different scenarios of how to move circle. GS becoming the forward or diagonal

Question: Why might we do this?

CPs, Communication, Confident, Speed

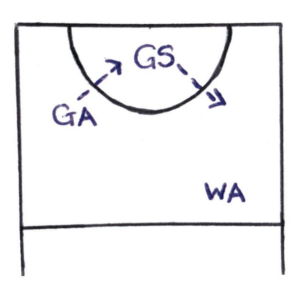

GA entry to a holding shooter:

1. Run the line to receive ball
2. Run the front to pull defence
3. Angles in and out to re-work

CPs: GA, speed and decision making. GS, strong hold, body angle open to post and ball

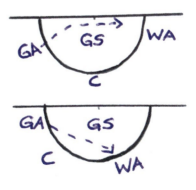

Hitting circle Edge:

1. Explain how to angle body on edge of circle to protect space and set up top and side, ball side. Practise swing and bounce.
CPs. Strong body position, Body angle, Ball placement

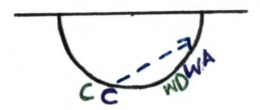

2. Work self to edge, using speed, agility, and body. 'F's job is to place 'A' on edge with ball placement. Work 6x then change

Progression:

1. Add a defender

CPs, Body angle, Communication, Strength, Speed, Take on the defender

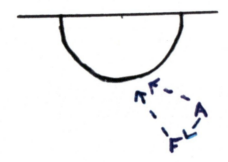

3. Work as a unit to attack the ball to circle edge and make 2 passes on the circle.
Question: How do we successfully work together?
CPs, Body angle, Communication, Strength, Speed, Take on the defender

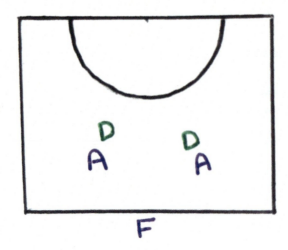

Samantha Griffin

4. WA drives and receives from WD, GS comes out and receives. WA drives to hit circle edge ball side for GS, whilst C hits top ball side. GS makes the decision who to pass to then drives to post. WA can choose to pull off the circle to create more space for C. Practice 6x using both WA and C. Defence start in active.

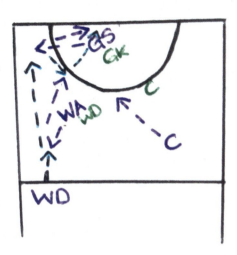

Progression:

1. Defensive become active
2. WA/C need to make 1 pass on circle edge before going to GS
3. Pass to WA when off the edge and play through
4. Add a GA/GD

CPs, Body angle, Communication, Strength, Speed, Take on the defender

Match Play:
Conditions:

1. One pass on circle edge
2. GS comes out to receive

Cool Down/Feedback

Attacking and Defensive Unit

Aim: To develop both the attackers and defender's connection within the goal circle. (This session will have sperate drills for each end)

Warm up: Split them off into units WA with shooters, WD with defenders split your C's equally. Each unit leads a warm-up, in a third each.

Attacking end:

Drill 1: GS/GA start by taking some time at the post, set a target of 50 goals in. Check shooting technique:

1. Stand with your feet hip width apart facing the post.
2. Hold the ball with your dominant hand. Position it under the ball with your fingertips relaxed.
3. Stabilise the ball with your other hand placed at the side of the ball. Do not apply to much pressure this is just there to support the ball it is not the hand to shoot with.
4. Hold the ball above your head with your arms stretched, with elbows slightly flexed, make sure your dominant arm is facing the post.
5. Sight the post and aim for the back of the ring.
6. Bend your knees and elbow then push up to release the ball making sure you follow through with your fingers on your dominate hand to ensure it is accurate.
7. Once you have released the ball run forward to collect the rebound, try and catch before the ball hits the floor.

WA/C go to the wall and complete 50 of each pass, if you do not have a wall pass together.

Drill 2: Cutting the cake

Shooters start out of the circle behind the post with WA/C spread around the circle with a ball stood at the end of a cone (can have more than 2). The first shooter enters the circle and drives to the first cone then comes back to post; they repeat this all the way around the circle moving out to each cone. WA/C can pass them the ball either on their drive out or back to post, the next shooter enters when the one ahead is at the top cone and must ensure when they are moving back to the post as they move forward. (always travelling one forward one back). Complete this starting on both sides of the circle twice each side.

CPs, Shooters- Body angle, Narrow base, Changing direction through pushing off on the outside foot, Vision, Timing

Mid court- Ball placement add touch to the ball

Samantha Griffin

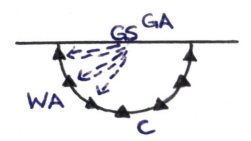

Drill 3: Circle rotation
Both shooters start within the circle with mid court around the edge. Shooters work for 6 passes before they can shoot. They can pass out and to each other. Make sure they are working together and not both moving into the same space at the same time. Rotate until everyone has had a go.
Progression: Add a defender (one of your mid court players or spare shooter)
CPs, Communication, Reading off, Timing, Passing accuracy

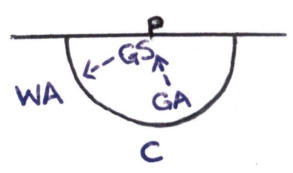

Drill 4: Setting up screens to promote options
DAAD
Ball starts at the top with WA 'A1' screens on 'D1' protecting the space for 'A2' to pop forward for ball, 'A1' remain on the screen for rebound position or a pass.

As WA swings the ball to C 'A2' pops top 'A1' drives the base to receive, 'A2' to post ensuring a good rebound position.

C passes to WA at the top 'A1' and 'A2' screen strong, 'A1' drives hard to receive the ball, 'A2' to post.

CPs, Strong body position, Angles, Commit to drive, Vision, Reading off each other

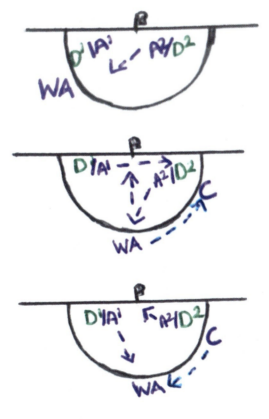

Progression: WA and C choose the set up they want to see from shooters by passing the ball. Shooters then must react to the situation

DADA-C/WA playing pockets, repositioning
'A1' to overload 'D1' protect post and wait for the swing. Both 'A1' and 'A2' protect own space and time opening body angle. C can choose which option to pass to.

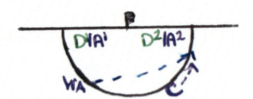

'A1' shut down 'D1' protect front space overload middle 'D2' 'A1' drive top, 'A2' post. WA/C choose who to pass to.

CPs, Strong body position, Angles, Commit to drive, Vision, Reading off each other

ADAD-GA lead the swing, shooter in
'A1' swing to C in the pocket, 'A2' turn and run at 'D1' pick up and screen to protect space, 'A1' drive front to overload 'D2' C chooses who to pass to if 'A2' becomes an option by opening out body and 'D2' commits to 'A1'

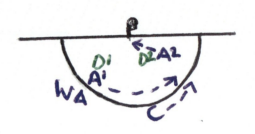

CPs, Strong body position, Angles, Commit to drive, Vision, Reading off each other

Samantha Griffin

Defensive end:

Drill 1: Variation in marking the shot

Defenders work in pairs with one playing the role of a shooter the other marking the shot. Practice different variations of applying pressure. Ensure defenders starts 3ft away from the shooters landing foot. Try each variation, ensure defender boxes out once the shooter has released the ball, so they are in the best position to gain the rebound, use the body to protect the space.

1. Static 3ft mark stretching as much as possible, try with one arm over the ball and then with two. Also try this with your other defender holding your dress to increase your stretch, be ready to react to the pass to the other shooter.

2. Jumping up to try and tip the ball as it is released or to apply pressure to the shooter. Time the jump to the 3 seconds or the release of the ball. Make sure you can turn once the shooter has released the ball and box out.

CPs, 3ft away, Balance, Stretching as tall as you can, Timing, Body strength

Drill 2: Cut the cake, anywhere ball

Defenders start out of the circle behind the post with WD/C spread around the circle with a ball (can have more than 2). The first defender enters the circle and drives to the first cone then comes back to post; they repeat this all the way around the circle moving out to each cone. WD/C can put an anywhere ball (high/low) into the circle at any point for them to pick up, the next defender enters when the one ahead is at the top cone and must ensure when they are moving back to the post as they move forward (always travelling one forward one back). Complete this starting on both sides of the circle twice each side.

CPs, Body angle, Narrow base, Reaction, Vision

Drill 3: Working together

Two defenders start within the circle, they need to work together to cover the space, one front, one back, left, and right. Communicate the switches when needed. C and WD can put the ball into the circle at any point to promote movement between the defenders to cover the space, they can also pass the ball to each other on the outside to change the defenders body angle. Defenders work for 10 balls

Progression:

1. Add one attacker within the circle for defenders to mark. 'A' is working to try and receive the ball, C and WD can try and pass to 'A' but also the space to ensure one defender is picking up the ball and the other protecting the post.

2. Add two attackers, defence try and position ADDA keeping both players high and wide within the circle or DADA dictating one 'A' high and connecting on the second 'A'

CPs, Communication, Body angle, Narrow base, Reaction, Vision

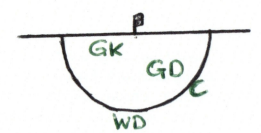

Drills 4: Scenarios

GD is pulled for obstruction out of the circle. GK needs to protect the post, get between the two shooters to encourage the ball to be received away from the post until GD can get back into play, once the ball has been passed GK needs to drop onto the player closest to post and GD picking up the player with the ball. WD can initial try and keep the GA from entering the circle but must react quickly, if not ensure they are pressuring the pass with a 3ft mark.

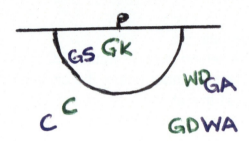

Preventing the GA entering the circle to leave the GK in a 1v1. GD starts off the body of the GA and times stepping up to prevent her entering the circle, GD needs to continue to work hard dictating the GA high and wide until the ball is forced into the GS. WD C also need to keep their players high and force the ball to be passed off the circle edge, apply 3ft mark when their opposing player has the ball.

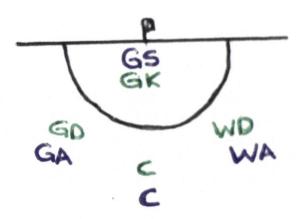

CPs, Communication, Body angle, Narrow base, Reaction, Vision

Conditioned Game: Bring players back together and set up against each other. Play the ball live anywhere from the top of the attacking third x6. After 6 debrief in units to discuss.

Samantha Griffin

Question: What did they do well? What can be improved?
Repeat x6 and add some starting from a CPA

Cool Down/Feedback

Options

Aim: Connection in attacking third, using different options

Warm up: Player led

1. Activation
2. Dynamic
3. Speed
4. Ball

Options: Complete 20 successful of each set

1. Lateral - forward	2. 2ⁿᵈ forward	3. 2ⁿᵈ forward - diagonal	4. Cut back

1. Lateral - forward   2. 2nd forward   3. 2nd forward - diagonal   4. Cut back

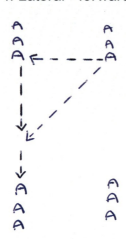 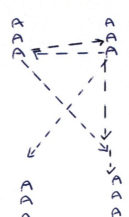 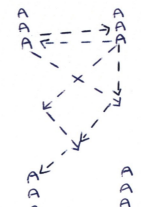 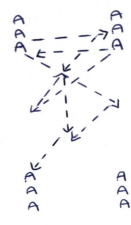

In drill one once you have passed the forward change to the queue parallel to you. Once you have worked to receive the forward join the opposite queue. Keep queues balanced.

Progression:

1. Add 2 defenders, attackers then need to make the correct decision on the options they provide and adapt to the defence.

CPs, Commitment to drive, Speed, Ball placement, Vision, Communication

In and out: Provide the forward and diagonal in the attacking third. Lateral and reset in the centre. Players rotate around all positions they play.

C gives a lateral ball to receive a forward

GA provides the next forward with WA diagonal, WD (L attack) to provide a reset/lateral. All players back their balls up, e.g. C, WA circle edge (keep it balanced), GA rebound

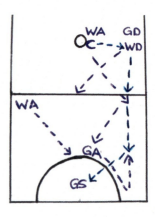

Complete 6x

Samantha Griffin

GA receives forward
WA receives diagonal
WD reset/lateral
Mix up (decision making)
Progression- Add defenders

Match Play

Cool down/Feedback

Strategies
Part 2

Restart Session

Aim: Retain basics / Stay focused on possession

Warm-Up: Player Led

Fitness/Agility/Skills:

Set 1: - Worker 10x Forward Drives
- 2x Sprints (1 third, there and back is 1)
- Feeder = Chest Pass until worker finished
- Change roles
Set 2: - Worker 10x Overs
- 2x Sprints (1 third, there and back is 1)
- Feeder = Overheads until worker finished
- Change roles
Set 3: - Worker 10x 45* Drive + Cut Back
- 2x Sprints (1 third, there and back is 1)
- Feeder = Right Hand until worker finished
- Change roles
Set 4: - 10x Anywhere's
- 2x Sprints (1 third - there and back is 1)
- Feeder = Left Hand
- Change roles

Conditioned Game: 5x Consecutive Goals
Split your group evenly in to each third, with shooters in each goal third.

1. Everyone in the third must have received the ball. Forward drives + release from over- head only.
2. Ball plays through each third. First time goal must be scored.
3. Work the ball back down.
4. Once the ball is out the third, complete x3 Burpees.
5. If had 5 attempts and do not complete it = 1 Suicide.

Conditioned Game: Possession/Melting Pot

1. Every 5 passes add a defender. Aim to get everyone in and keep the ball for 30seconds.
2. Conditions – ball released from above head – forward drives.
3. If "D" intercepts change roles.
4. Continue until both teams have completed.

CPs, Forward drives, Decision making, Accurate passing, Reading off, Communication

Samantha Griffin

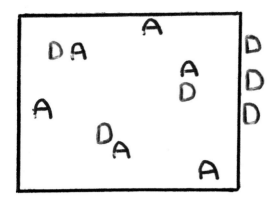

Match Play: 4 x 7 mins
Stats for: -Backlines to halfway
-Centre to Goal

Cool Down/Feedback

Vision

Aim: Developing Vision

Warm-Up: Player led

1. Activation
2. Dynamic
3. Speed
4. Ball

Agility/Ball Work: In groups of 3 complete 4x each
CPs, Body Angle, Fast Feet, Vision

Drill 1: Body Angle
Player holds up different coloured cones for 'D' to call out, whilst 'F' is feeding anywhere for 'D' to react too. Work for 6 feeds, change roles.
CP's, Open body angle, Fast feet, Vision

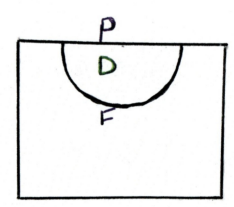

Drill 2: 'D' is now competing against 'A', who is aiming to beat (GK) to the ball and get to the post. (GK) 'D', aim is to still get the ball and protect the post. Work for 6 feeds, then change roles.
CP's, Strength, Dictate, Body angle, Vision

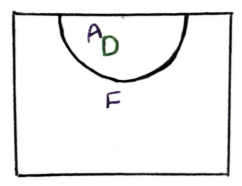

Drill 3: Unit defence 2v1 'D' work together to protect post. Force the long shot. Shooter works for x6 goals or defence x3 turnover.
CP's, Communication, Footwork, Body Angles, Vision

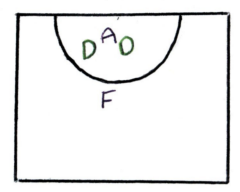

Drill 4: 2v2 focus on protecting the post. 'A' works for 6 passes before they can shoot. Defence intercept x3 or force error.
CP's, Communication, Strength, Vision.

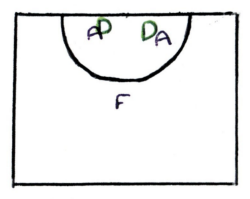

Drill 5: Stage 1 defender pulled out for obstruction.
What is 'D2' job? What is 'D1' job?
Question: How do we become a successful unit?

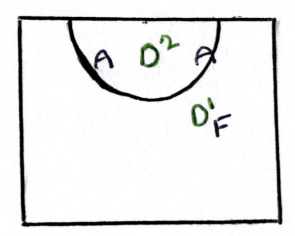

Conditioned Game:

Work for sets of 6 balls WA, C offer from 'F1' they must hit circle edge to feed. GS thinks about where the ball is, times movement, receives and passes ball to GA. WA, C offer from 'F2' repeat, GA passes ball back to 'F1'. GS can shoot on the 6th ball, players rotate.

Progression:

1. Add GA into play
2. WA/C must make one pass between each other on circle edge
3. 'F1' becomes WD with 'F2' WA, attack must rest the ball once to WD before scoring

CPs, Communication, Definite moves, Reading off

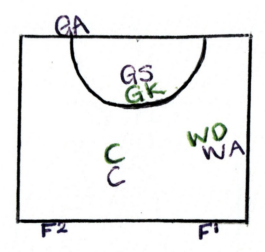

Match Play:

Conditions: 1 pass between WA/C on circle edge, 1 reset pass to WD or GD before scoring

Cool Down/Feedback

Samantha Griffin

Hitting Circle Edge

Aim: Taking on defender to hit circle edge.

Warm-Up: Player led

1. Activation
2. Dynamic
3. Speed
4. Ball

Agility/Fitness:
1- Sprint Forward
2- Side Steps Back
3- Sprint Across
Aim to catch the person in front
Stop when back at the cone you started on
2nd time change direction
Repeat X4

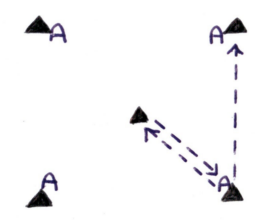

Drill 1: Opening out
'A2' Drives forward to receive from 'F', passes with outside hand to the way she is running, opens the inside shoulder to clear around the top cone, runs down to the bottom corner and repeats from the other side. 'A1' follows with both players timing to work together. Work for 6 balls change the 'F' repeat until all fed.

CPs, Body angles, Vision, Speed, Footwork

Drill 2: Hitting Circle Edge

"A" drives forward to 'F' receives ball looks forward before passing back then uses speed and body to hit the circle edge, practicing cutting in front and behind.

Feeders job is to put 'A' on the edge, pass to GS to score and repeat x6

2 Groups use half circle each

CPs, Body angle, Speed, Vision, Agility to step around a defender cut towards the edge, knowledge of when and how to stop and hold position before attacking to the edge.

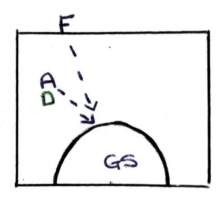

Drill 3: Swing

'A' work to circle edge, must make 2 passes on circle edge before passing to GS

Practise, Swing + Bounce (break down) repeat x6

CPs, Body angle, Vision between WA and C, Decision making between moving and holding, Vary release and type of delivery.

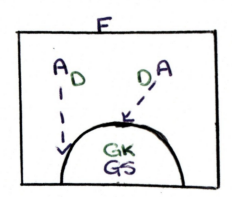

Conditioned Game: Getting to edge and working as a Mid-Court team

Part 1 staged. 'A' release to GS as she comes out, should then try, and get ball side if not come off the edge to become an option or 'A2' should be ball side. GS works to get to post and re-receive to shoot.

Progressions:

1. Keep set up (staged) WA and C make 5 passes before passing to GS, can reset to 'F'
2. Take out staged set up
3. Add a GA

Question what should the mid court be thinking about?

1. Can I pass and cut myself? Is there a line to the circle edge?
2. Does my mid-court teammate have a better line? Do they know you are creating space for them?
3. If I cannot get a line to the circle edge, when do I come off?
4. How can we work together to overload defenders?
5. What if neither of us can get the ball side?

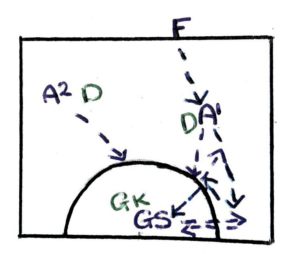

Match Play:

Conditions:

1. WA/C must feed from circle edge
2. Mid court make one pass between them before passing into the circle
3. Mid court reset to WD and then attack circle edge

Cool Down/Feedback

Robust Player applied on Defensive Set Ups

Aim: Remaining strong when defending the opposition CP

Warm-Up: Player led, except when the ball comes in. Using the entire court drive and clear timed for 1min no errors. Add in balls (up to 3). Conditions, forward drive, touch an outside line once thrown the ball.

Fitness: Speed/ball skills

100 chest passes - against wall

30 secs as many sprints as possible (each cone 1 point)

100 overhead passes

30 secs

100 right hand shoulder passes

30 secs

100 left hand shoulder passes

30 secs

100 right hand close range - one leg

30 secs

100 left hand close range - one leg

(There and back is 1 point - beat score each time)

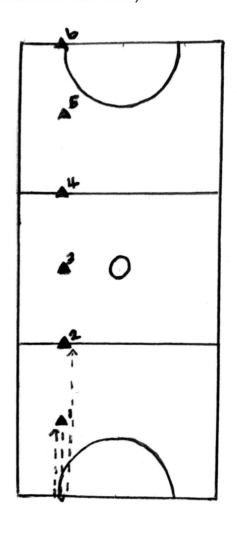

Drill 1: 'A' working to receive the ball in box

'D1' applying pressure to 'A', trying to stop her receiving. 'D2' has tackle pad to nudge 'A' when taking the ball

Progress:

1. 'D2' apply pressure at any time

CPs, Definite drives, Balanced landing, Catch with two hands

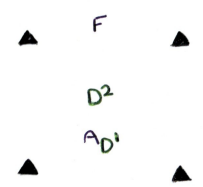

Drill 2: 'A' must enter through first of cones where both 'D1' and 'D2' have tackle pads to knock 'A'. 'A' then needs to enter through second cones and work to receive ball against 2 defenders. Work for 4 attempts each, change roles.

Progression:

1. Move the cones closer together

CPs, Speed, Definite drives, Balanced landing, Catch with two hands

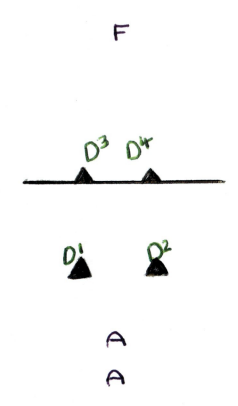

Defensive Set Ups:

1ˢᵗ phase High and Wide: 2ⁿᵈ phase stopping depth

1- C up on ball on an angle

2- WD/GD straight out 1ˢᵗ phase and then play to recovery position 2ⁿᵈ phase.

3- WA/GA flooding 1ˢᵗ phase

4- C stay on ball to delay C run on 2ⁿᵈ phase

CPs, Early prep, body angle, strength, dictate, communication

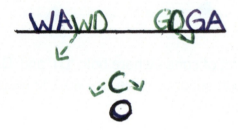

1ˢᵗ phase Squeeze: 2ⁿᵈ phase stopping depth

1- WD/GD be strong and overload middle

2- C to cover middle

3- WA/GA work hard to stop back up

CPs, Early prep, body angle, strength, dictate, communication

2v1

1- 2 on 1 does not receive the ball - be aggressive over line and step to space to dictate

Samantha Griffin

2- 1 on 1 face away from ball or wide + contest

CPs, Early prep, body angle, strength, dictate, communication

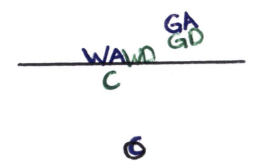

Zero Phase

Everyone on early, stop opposition from setting up

Force the error on first phase

CPs, Early prep, body angle, strength, dictate, communication

Question: How can attack get involved?

1 - WA/GA forcing wide + high or keeping from entering Centre third- apply defence early

2- GS step up and pick up GD to delay getting to line

3- WA/GA double WD.

CP'S: Early prep, communication, strength, dictate

Match Play:
Conditions:
1: white - 2 points turn over to goal
   black - 1 centre to goal
   6 mins change
2: 51-51 40 secs x3
   30 secs x3
   20 secs x3
   10 secs x3
3: Losing 52-51
   Winning 52-51
4: Win by 2 ends the game

Cool down/Feedback

Samantha Griffin

Zero Phase

Aim: Zero phase A/D, reaction

Warm-Up: Player led

1. Activation
2. Dynamic
3. Speed
4. Ball

Reaction: 'F' has two tennis balls held out. 'F' drops one at a time, 'A' must pick up within one bounce or less.
CPs, Fast feet, Vision

Progression: 'F' moves further away from 'A'

Reaction 2: 'D' leads first, gaining the opportunity to set up in front of 'A'. Coach calls colour the first player to the coloured cone wins. Repeat x6 then change 'A' to leader x6
CPs, Body strength, Angle, Footwork, Speed

Drill: Zero Phase
'A' sets up in between 2 markers 'D' sets up early dictating 'A' away from the ball. 'A' needs to cross the solid line before they can receive the ball. After each one reset between the cones. Continue until 'D' intercepts/forces 4 errors.
Flip the drill to 'A' setting up early as an easy way to receive the ball, drive straight x4 each
CPs, Reaction, Body angle, Feet

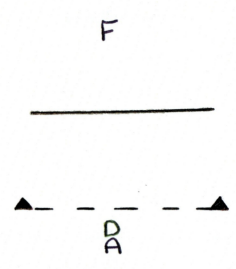

Question: How can zero phase help you when defending? How can it be utilised when attacking?

Conditioned Game: Attack v Defence

Attack enter from gate, 3 players at a time attempt to score by passing into the box. Whoever catches the ball to score must run back with the ball staying in the area and must go back through the gate, the next 3 attackers can then enter. Aim is to score as many points in 1 minute.

Defenders enter from the sides 3 players Attempt to apply zero phase, discuss at half time. in at once, can change at any point, defenders are not allowed in the gate or box. If they intercept the ball, they must put it on the floor.

3 attempts each, change roles after each attempt
CPs, Communication, Reaction, Decision making

Progression: If 'A' score run to create a CPA play to goal

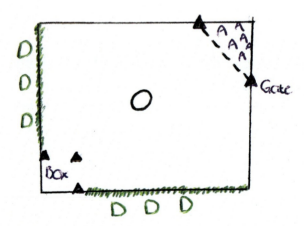

Match Play: Attempt to apply zero phase, discuss at half time.

Cool down/Feedback

Samantha Griffin

Zero Phase

Aim: Applying zero phase/early prep as an attacker and defender into a game situation.

Warm up: Player led

Question: What is zero phase?

How do we apply it?

Benefits using it as a defender and attacker?

Where can we use it? (A&D)

Drill 1: Competing with the set up
'P1' & 'P2' compete to set up zero phase in the box. 'F' shouts play, both players drive out the box competing for an anywhere ball, 'F' must play the ball in front of the players. Change 'F' every 4, continue until everyone competed for 4 against each other.
CPs, Quick feet, Body angle, Strength, Speed to ball

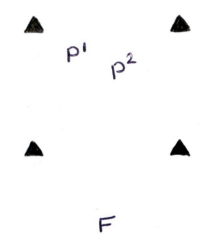

Drill 2: 2v1
Two players now work together v one other to ensure one of them wins the ball. Repeat x4 then rotate the feeder.
CPs, Communication, Job role, Feet, Angle, Strength, Vision

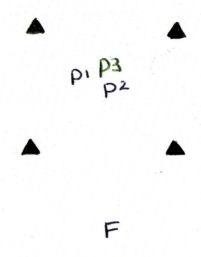

Drill 3: 2v2

Work as a unit to win the ball, play two passes out of the box to gain 1 point. First to 3 points change the feeder and pairings.

CPs, Communication, Job role, Feet, Angle, Strength, Vision

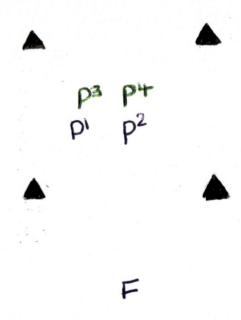

Question: In a match when might we be in a 2v1/2v2 situation that zero phase can help us from an A&D point?

Conditioned Game: Live Ball
1. Start with ball thrown in at one end team that gets it first attacks it
2. Start with a player throwing the ball out of the court to create a side-line/goal line
3. Take some from CP

Cool down/Feedback

Samantha Griffin

Dealing with a tall GS/GK

Aim: To learn different ways of how to play against a tall GS and GK

Dealing with:	Solution:
Tall GS	Off the body and turnover early
Long balls - forward thinking	Dictating
1 over 1st phase	2v1
Risk takers in defence	High work rate
High scorers	Apply pressure through consistency

Warm-Up: Player Led

Game: Keep ball for 20 passes centre third.

Catch in the box 2pts, C circle 5pts, no restrictions on 3ft mark.

Progression - break out at 20 to goal

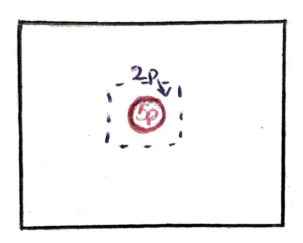

Agility drills:

1: Hit 4 cones drive forward, 'F' vary ball

    X6 and change

    Add defender

CPs, Angles, Change of speed

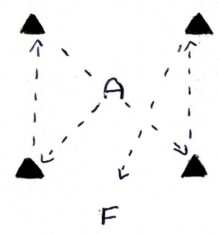

2: Smaller box 'A' works for 6 consecutive passes
    Start out the box - drive in, 3 sec rule applies
CPs, Strength, Commitment

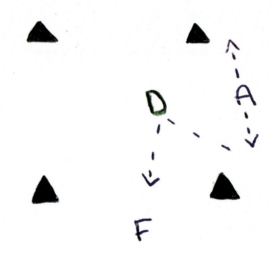

Defending:
Defending off the body
GK comes off the body to intercept the ball
Add another "F" defender must reposition to ball
Work for 5 then change
CPs, Fast feet, Open body, Timing, Commit

Samantha Griffin

GD take intercept

GK dictates GS towards the ball, GD open out body angle, run feet to take the ball, if miss, GK pick up GA on entry, GD on the front of GS.

CPs, Fast feet, Open body, Timing, Commit

WD off body 1ˢᵗ phase

Still dictate to set up the angle, run hard at the ball

CPs, Fast feet, Open body, Timing, Commit

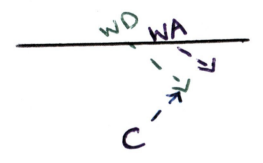

Attack:

Moving Circle

From C, GS plans to come out open circle for GA, rework if the first ball is not on.

CPs, Strong drives, Timing, Reading off

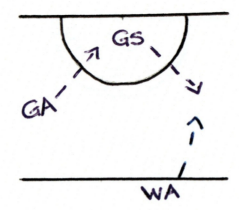

GS to always hold front and move on to the ball
Start holding, then move, centre court to wait for GS to move onto the ball, GA run the goal line, keep pulling for each other until working the ball to post.
CPs, Body angle, Timing, Strength

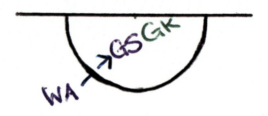

Match Play: Bonus points
1. Interception from off the body
2. GS receiving outside the circle

Cool down/Feedback

Samantha Griffin

Reading Off

Aim: Timing and reading off each player.

Warm-Up: Player led

1. Activation
2. Dynamic
3. Speed
4. Ball

Drill 1: Turning out
1. 'A' drives out at 45* (still forward not flat) turns out and passes to opposite 'F' continues to work for 12 balls.
2. Two 'A's working together on the same drill need to work in time.
CPs, Strong drive, Land on outside foot, fully turn the body before passing, Single hand pass with your inside hand once tuned e.g. drive right, land right, pass with right, Timing

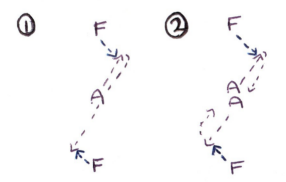

Conditioned Game: Two teams, Two sides
Each team needs to play the ball from one end to the other, complete 6x successfully (to goal) on both sides. Start with conditions:
1. Can only receive the ball once, must drive forward, must back up as far as you can e.g. WA to circle edge
2. Add in a lateral to GK
3. Add in a reset to WD
4. Once GK, GD have attacked their ball they then move across to defend. Then becomes first team to 6 goals.
5. GD/WD bring ball out high, C clears, WA comes through

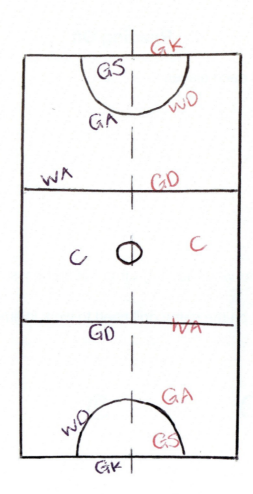

Question: When do we release the ball?
- When do we start to drive?
- What should happen before drive?
- How many options should we have for every ball?

Court Set Ups:
5x from goal line
5x from over third line/side-line
5x from centre
5x from live play
Question: position / preparation

Match Play

Cool down/Feedback

Samantha Griffin

Strategies
Part 3

Moving forward to the ball under fatigue

Aim: Forward to ball, improving decision making at speed and under pressure/fatigue

Warm-Up:
   1- Activation
   2- Tig with dynamic movement
      Set 1, 3
      T1- Lunges
      T2 - Squats
      T3 - Burpee
      Set 2, 4
      T1 - Knees to chest (tuck jump)
      T2 - Mountain Climbers
      T3 - Star Jump

3 players on if tug exit third to complete exercise
`A` allowed in boxes for 3 secs cannot get tug. 30 secs each set (court set up below)

3- 2 teams, Defence v Attack
30 seconds to score as many points as possible by passing into the box. Cannot score in the same box twice in a row. 'D' is not allowed in the box. If 'D' turns the ball over, they have to put the ball on the floor. 2 sets each. Allow for each team to feedback in between.

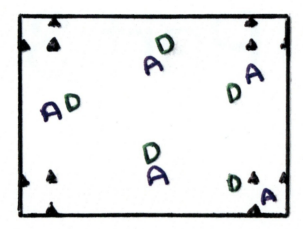

Reaction/Speed:
Feeders start with 2 tennis balls, 'A' hands on top of 'F' out at chest height.
'F' drops one ball, 'A' needs to pick up before bounce, 'F' drops second ball
Coach calls number 1 or 2 for 'A's to sprint halfway and hold the ball above head. Work for 6x sprints + change.
CPs, Quick feet, Vision

Samantha Griffin

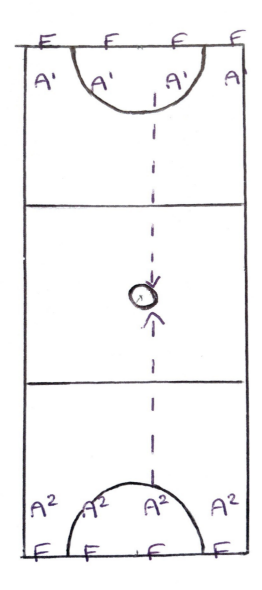

Drill 1: Forward to ball
'A' must work to receive 10 passes, can only drive forward to receive the ball, 'F's can move around the outside but only one on each line, 'F' can pass to each other.
CPs, Definite drives, Speed, Vision

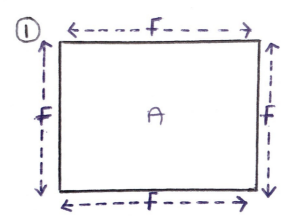

Progression 1: Add a defender

Question: As the attacker what types of movement/set ups can we do to get free from the defender?

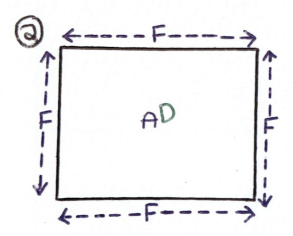

Progression 2: 2v1

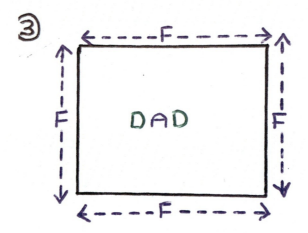

Progression 3: 2v2

Attack work for 20 balls consecutive, Defence communicate to work together successfully to challenge the attack.

CPs, Meet ball, body angle, Prelim movement, Communication, Speed, Ball placement

Question: What can we do to improve?

What has been successful?

Samantha Griffin

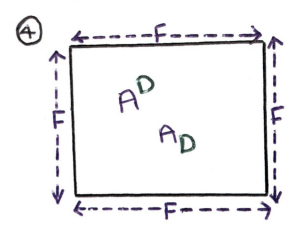

Conditioned Game:

Ball must travel through all boxes, defenders not allowed in the box. Work to goal - 3 consecutive only 2 players from each team allowed in the circle. 3 burpees every error.

CPs, Communication, Vision, Definite drive, Timing

Question: What do we need to do to be successful?

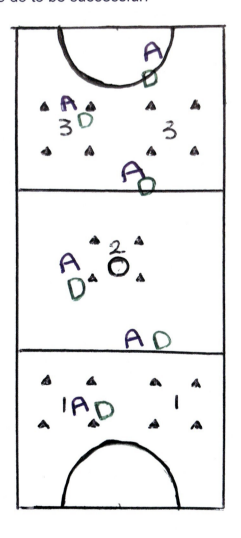

Match Play

Cool down/Feedback

Defensive Set Ups

Aim: To be able to work as a unit in defence to promote different setups to force errors/ interception.

Warm-Up: Player led

Drill: Near Side, engaging together

'D1' dictates and communicate to 'D2', 'D2' arms over and changes angle to cut off 'A'. Work for 6 interceptions then change roles.

CPs, Communication, Body angle, Footwork, Reaction, Vision, Timing

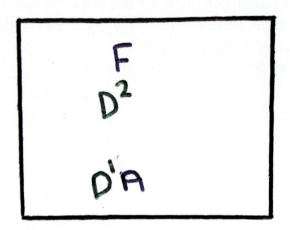

Side-line / Back-line/ Penalty Plays:
1. Overload one side, anything else dictate far side

Set up different scenarios and apply the same concept

CPs, Communication, Body angle, Footwork, Reaction, Vision, Timing, everyone do a job

Samantha Griffin

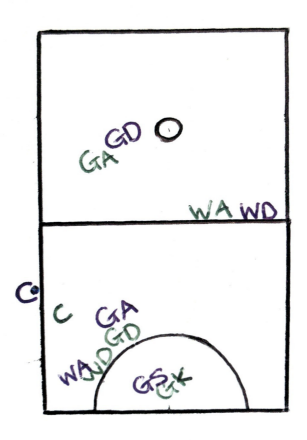

2. Promoting the intercept

Long ball into pockets/ long ball through court.

CPs, Communication, Body angle, Footwork, Reaction, Vision, Timing, everyone do a job

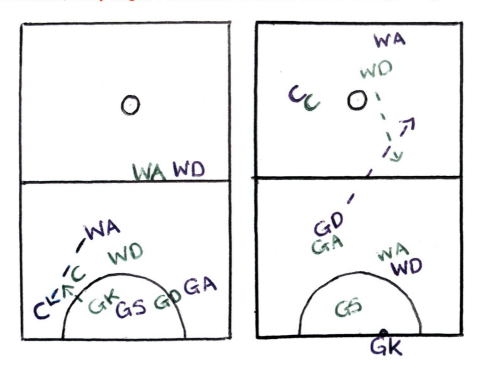

3. Force high and together or wide (Far Side at the other end of the court)

CPs, Communication, Body angle, Footwork, Reaction, Vision, Timing, everyone do a job

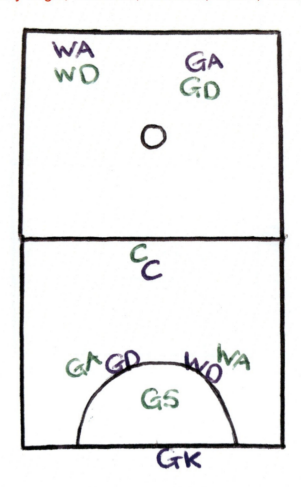

Recap from previous session: Centre pass defence set up

1. Wide and high allow 1st phase
2. 2v1 - figure out who receives most WA or GA
3. Squeeze
4. Zero Phase

Match Play: Apply different set ups, keep stopping and starting to give feedback

Cool down/Feedback

Samantha Griffin

Near Side/Far Side

Aim: Applying Near Side/ Far Side defence to game situations.

Warm-Up: Player led

1. Activation
2. Dynamic
3. Speed
4. Ball

Agility: Two thirds same set up coloured cone boxes, split into two teams.
Players start fast feet - coach calls
- left, right, up, down
- colour - last to box = 3 burpees
- ball 20 left, 20 right shoulder
- play first team to make 3 points
Scoring in the boxes, cannot score in the same box twice.
CPs, Body angle, Footwork, Vision, Strength, Communication

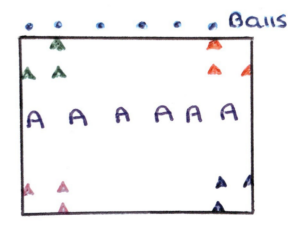

Near Side:
'D1' needs to keep 'A' the same side of the line as the ball and try to dictate as close to the ball as possible to connect with 'D2' work until defence intercept 6.
CPs, Body angle, Footwork, Vision, Strength, Communication.

Far side:
'D1' needs to keep 'A' away from the ball, opposite side of the line to 'F'. Work for 6 errors/ interceptions

CPs, Body angle, Footwork, Vision, Strength, Communication.

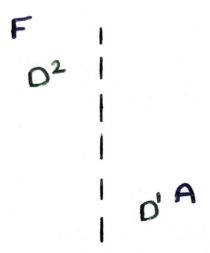

Side-line Set Ups:
Play through different set ups, each one 6 times, discuss as a team. What set ups are successful for you? What set ups do not play to your strengths?
Think about what you want to achieve
All near/far side = overload
Use both styles
Everyone needs to do a job
CPs, Body angle, Footwork, Vision, Strength, Communication.

Samantha Griffin

Three set up examples:

Match Play: Create some side-line set ups throughout the court. Discuss at breaks.

Cool down/Feedback

Consistency

Aim: Remaining consistent

Warm-Up: Roller ball, two teams aiming to score over the goal line by rolling a tennis ball across the line. Can take 3 steps with the ball, ball must stay on the ground. Can intercept with hands only no kicking.

Agility/Speed: Races
Set up 4 cones zig zagged at least 1m apart from the goal line to third line. With a larger cone ahead in line with the centre circle.

Split into 3 teams, start behind a section each. Aim is to race to knock down the top cone.

Coach calls numbers for them to hit and change direction before getting to the top cone. Complete 4x each.

CPs, Speed. Vision, Pushing of the outside foot

Passing / Forward drives:
Teams play the ball x5 through court, last player throws off the wall

Conditions
1. Prelim movement then forward drives only to receive the ball
2. Outward turn
3. Shoulder pass
4. Any errors start again

Progression:
1. Shooter at the end must get a goal, if misses re-start
2. Can cut back/forward to receive the ball
3. Add Defenders
CPs, Communication, Reading off, Passing accuracy, Timing, Definite movement

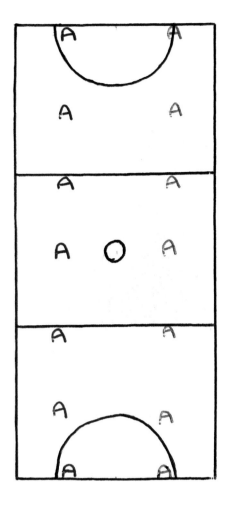

Centre pass to goal: Averaging 12 centres a quarter
- Sets of 12x2
- Take stats, record mistakes why
- If defence intercept play ball halfway for a point
- Every point defence get, attack owe in suicides. Defence points for turnover, forced error

Defensive back line: (attacking) Averaging 6
- Sets of 6x2
- Conditions the same as above

Match Play
1- 2 x 7 mins Purple v Blue
Blue centre passes = 1pt
Purple winning ball = 2pt
Change roles in 2nd round of 7 mins
2- Match stops when a team goes up by 2 points

Cool down/Feedback

Long and short option

Aim: Providing a short and long option immediately after the intercept

Warm up: Player led

1. Activation
2. Dynamic
3. Speed
4. Ball

Drill 1: 'A' keep possession within the box, can pass out to 'F'. 'D' working to intercept the ball, once they have intercepted, they pass to 'F' who must adjust wide to the box. 'D's must then work together to provide a long and short option. Work for 3, then change roles.
CPs, Communication, Vision, Speed, Angles

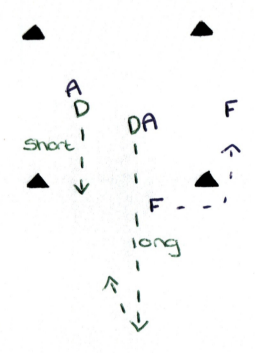

Conditioned Game: WA & C work to make 8 passes in the box can use GS on the outside, if they make 8, they can continue to attack to goals. GD, WD aim is to intercept the ball, they must off load to GK first then ensure they provide one long one short option for GK then continue to attack the ball to goal. First team to score 3 wins then change over which team starts off defending.
CPs, Communication, Decision making, Timing

Samantha Griffin

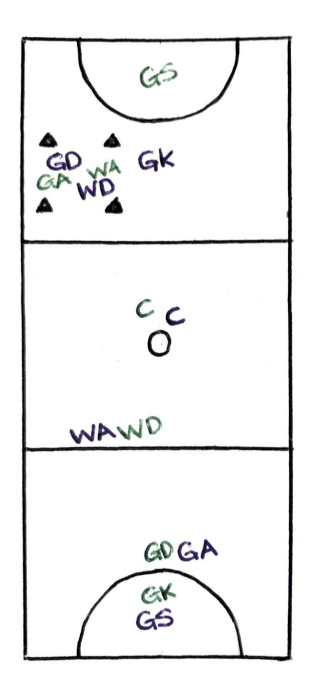

Match Play:
Following an interception get the players to recognise who is providing the long and the short.
Take stats on intercepts to goal.

Cool down/Feedback

Transition

Aim: Decision making, reaction A-D-A, circle rotation.

Warm-Up: Player led

1. Activation
2. Dynamic
3. Speed
4. Ball

Agility and ball drill:
'A' Drives straight to receive from the top 'F' passes back then goes around 'F' starting on their left, 'A' then drives to next 'F' and repeats to all. Once everyone understands the movement, 'A' can start to work at the same time, second 'A' can start when the one ahead comes around the top 'F'. Work for 1 set of 3 reps before changing roles.

Question: What do you have to consider in this drill?
CPs, Definite drive, Body angle, Timing, Accurate passing, Footwork

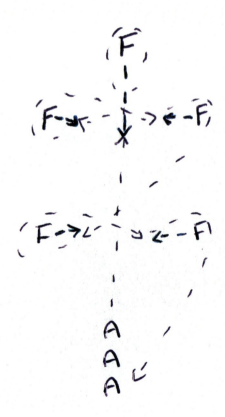

Conditioned game:
Only give rules, empower players decisions - 2 teams of 6
1- Only have 1min to score as many points as possible by catching the ball in the box
2- 3 'A' in at once, 3 'D' in at once

Samantha Griffin

3- Once scored can run back with the ball

4- 'A' must enter + reset after every point through the gate

5- 'D' can only enter through side lines.

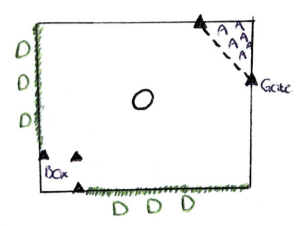

Transition:

Only give rules: 'A' works the ball across the side-line then exit the third with the next 'A' entering, 'D' needs to intercept the ball to become 'A'

3x teams of 4

1- Play until 1 team receives 3 points for working the ball over the line.

Team feedback

2- First team to 5 points, winning team set forfeit

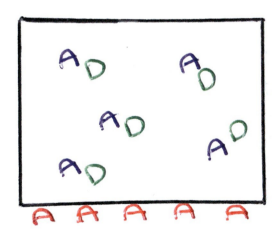

Match Play: Changing speed, players either pass on one second release, two second, three second, coach shout the changes. Discuss when is the best time to pass quickly and when is the time to slow the play down.

Cool down/Feedback

Options

Aim: Providing 3 options (Players making decisions)

Warm up: Player led

1. Activation
2. Dynamic
3. Speed
4. Ball

Forward option:
'A2' gives lateral receives forward
'A5' prelim then to forward
'A6' works forward
Work for 10 change sides using the diagonal, repeat x10
Players then work for 20 and can add diagonal
CPs, Timing, Ball placement, Definite drives

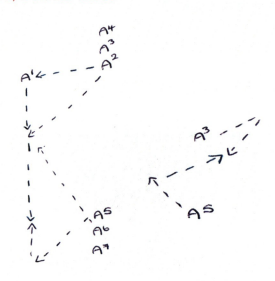

Fake forwards give the lateral:
'A2' gives lateral works forward
'A1' gives lateral receives forward choose to pass forward or diagonal
'A5' and 'A6' read off
CPs. Reading off, Communication

Samantha Griffin

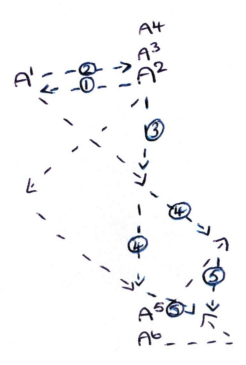

3 Options: Put up on flip chart
Start with using option 1, on left side of the diagram once they are consistent get them to play it out in the opposite direction. Then give them the power to change which option they pass too. Repeat with right side of the diagram. Continue practicing until players can successfully make their own decisions in providing different options.
CPs, Timing, Ball placement, Definite drives, Communication (reading off)

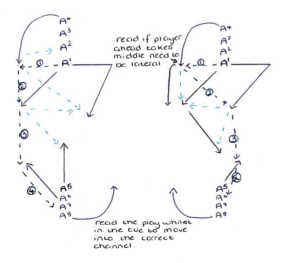

Match Play:
Ensure throughout the game, players are providing three options for every ball.

Cool down/Feedback

Being Efficient

Aim: To be efficient as an individual and a team.

Warm-Up: Player led

1. Activation
2. Dynamic
3. Speed
4. Ball

Agility/Fitness: Races
Coach calls colours set up in a square - then race to knock over large cone
CPs, Body angle, Speed, Vision

Forward Drives:
Complete 2 sets of 10 forwards in pairs

Game: Split into 3 thirds - ball travels through each to goal + back until complete 5x consecutive x2
Conditions
- Every player in the third receives ball
- Forward drives only
- Complete 3x burpees after receiving ball
- If shooter misses begin again

Progression: Add defenders
CPs, Definite drives, Timing, Communication, Passing accuracy

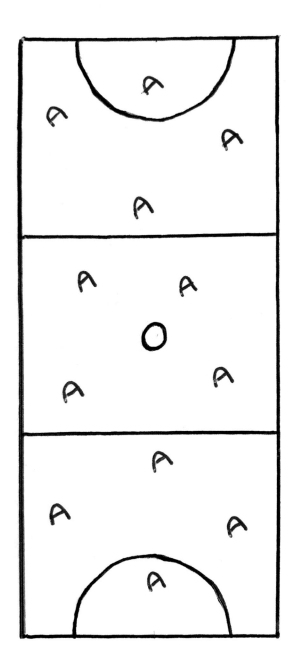

Set Ups:
- Centre pass to goal 2x6 consecutive
- Back line out 2x6 consecutive (change positions on 2nd set)
- If the team makes errors, follow below punishments in order
- 1st error=30second sprints
- 2nd error=1min wall sit
- 3rd error=10 burpees
- 4th error=1min plank

Take stats + break down where needed.

Match Play: Take stats of CPA and BL

Team ends the game if they win by 3 clear goals

Cool down/Feedback

Essentials

Movement

Aim: Demonstrate essential movement skills whilst working at a high intensity.

Warm up: All players moving around the court, one tennis ball. The player with the tennis ball changes the movement. Keep passing the ball around.

Agility circuit: Each station 1 min, change 'F' at 30 seconds

1. 'D' moves in a figure of 8, accelerates onto ball, like taking an intercept.

2. 'A' drive forward receive, move forward for drop ball, across for a chest, back space for high ball. Pass back to 'F' each time.

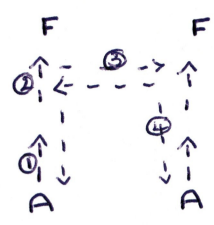

3. Anywhere in pairs, 'F' feeds the ball in quickly, 'A' communicates.

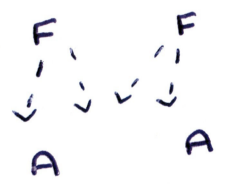

4. 'A' changing direction at each cone, whilst keeping body angle open to 'F' who can put the ball in at any point.

5. 'D' completes figure of 8 between cones, then drives out left to receive and then across receive. 'F' passes the ball in front.

6. 'A' up and over, sidestep then sprint forward to receive, pass back, 'F' drops the ball, change roles.

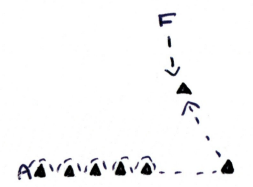

Samantha Griffin

7. 'A' changes of direction, pushing off on the outside foot. Move around top coning opening angle to 'F' who passes a high ball into back space.

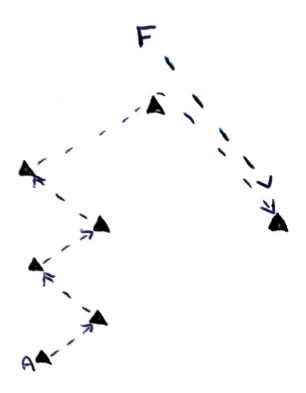

8. 'A' moves to every cone returning to post each time. 'F' can pass the ball in at any time.

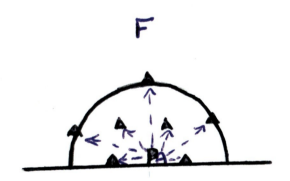

9. 'A' works to each cone keeping body angle open, 'F' passes to 'A' at each cone ensuring ball placement in front and passes sent in time so 'A' is not waiting.

Skills: Clear and drive

1. 'A' must drive into the box on a forward drive to receive the ball, once passed the ball 'A' must go out the box before re-entering. Work for 20 passes. Errors = restart.

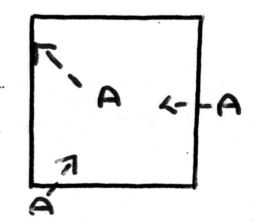

2. 'A' with ball can only pass to the second option in the box, working on re-offering. Ensure its not the same players receiving all the time, players need to communicate.

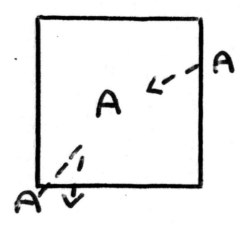

Samantha Griffin

3. 'A's' must make 10 consecutive passes, same rules as drill one (now have one defender in the box),

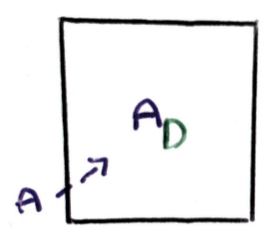

4. 2 'A' v 2 'D'- 'A's' must make 10 consecutive passes, same rules as above.

CPs, Commitment to drives, Speed, Timing, Communication, Angles, ball release points and placement.

Conditioned game:
'A' attacking ball from 1 box to the next, cannot score in the same box twice in a row. Change roles when 'D' intercept or cause error. 'D' not allowed in the box. Work for 2mins.
CPs, Communication, Decision making, Vision, Definite drives

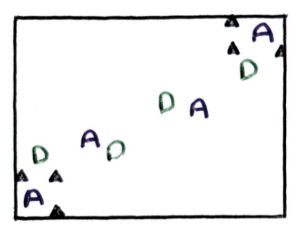

Match Play: Look at the essentials, footwork, balance, ball placement, body angle. How are they?

Cool Down/Feedback

Possession

Aim: Meeting the ball and keeping possession

Warm up: Player led

1. Activation
2. Dynamic
3. Speed
4. Ball

Drills: Work for 10 consecutives, then change roles

1. Forward Drive	2. Backspace	3. 45* outward turn	4. 45* cut back

CPs, Definite drives, Straight lines, Ball placement, Body angle (correct turn on the cut back inward)

Progression: Choose any movement to receive 10 consecutive v two defenders

CPs, Commit to movement, Prelim moves, Ball placement, Intensity, Timing

Conditioned game: Drive and clear/Possession

1. Drive and clear 1 min no error, all forward drive, once passed the ball run out and touch a line to clear, no defenders
2. Every 5 passes defender enters. Get all 'D' in and keep the ball for 1 min

CPs, Communication, Intensity, Angles, Commitment to drives, Decision making, Vision

Samantha Griffin

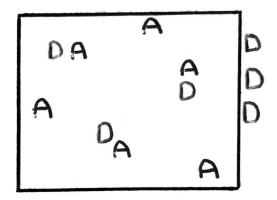

Half court:

Challenge: attack need to make 6 consecutive centre passes to goal.

Defence need to make 6 consecutive backlines to attacking third line.

Every error= fitness punishment

1- 5x burpees

2- 5x press ups

3- 5x sprints

4- 1 min wall sit

5- 1min plank

Cool Down/Feedback:

Question: What do you think our main aim will be when attacking?

Attacking angles

Aim: Being able to change body angle to help get free when attacking.

Warm up: Player led

1. Activation
2. Dynamic
3. Speed
4. Ball

Agility fitness: In partners, one player wall sits, whist player two sprints. Work for 1 minute change and continue for 6 minutes

Zone ball:
Feeders call out a number sequence. 'A' must successfully receive passes from 'F' in the zones relating to that number.

Progressions

1. Add 'D'
2. If defender intercepts roles change
3. Add a second defender

CPs, Body angle, Ball placement, Reaction, Change of direction

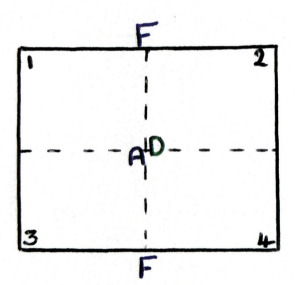

Cross the pond:
Attackers need to work together to work the ball across the 'Pond' to score a goal.
If 'D' force error they become 'A', first team to 3 points wins. 'D' only allowed in their area.
CPs, Communicate, Definite drives, Ball placement

Samantha Griffin

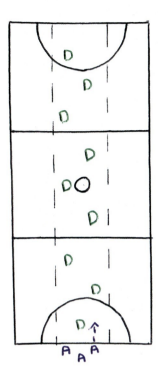

YoYo:

1. Attackers in area 1 try to score as many goals as they can in 30 seconds. After a goal is scored ball restarts with feeder
2. Defenders aim to intercept and transition back to feeder
3. Area 2 repeats
4. Both 'A's' work together no area split (full court) to see how many goals they can now score

CPs, Communicate, Definite drives, Ball placement, Speed, Reaction

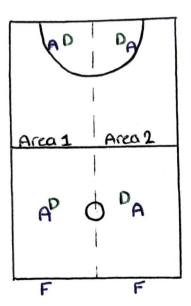

Match play

Cool down/Feedback

Defensive principles, dictating high + wide

Warm up: Player led

1. Activation
2. Dynamic
3. Speed
4. Ball

Agility: Defensive movement

D: 1. picks up drop ball
    2. Intercepts over
    3. Takes 45 degrees
    4. Intercepts straight ball
    Repeat x3 = 1 set complete 3 sets each

CPs, Speed, Body angle, Quick feet

Drill 1: 'A' working for 10 balls, if they land near the top cones, they get 1 point, back cone 2 points. 'D' needs to work hard to limit points. Work for 6 passes, change roles. Repeat twice each, see if you can beat your first score.

CPs, Body angle, Footwork, Timing the intercept

Samantha Griffin

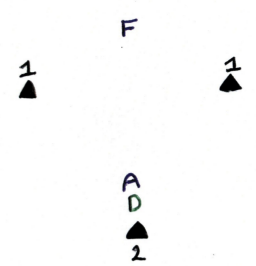

Question: Why would we rather 'A' receives the ball at the top cones than the bottom?

Drill 2: 'A' aims to receive the ball between the cones on circle edge. 'A' can keep passing to 'F' before timing when to take on 'D'. 'D' needs to keep 'A' high off the circle edge whilst timing it correctly to take the intercept. Work until 'D' makes 6 intercepts or keeps 'A' off the circle.
Progression: 'F' can become active, 'D' then needs to practice dropping off 'A' for the back and up intercept
CPs, Timing, Running feet, Strong body angle

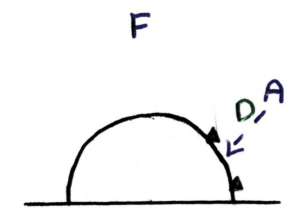

Drill 3: 3v2, 'A' aim to attack the ball from the top of the box to the bottom to get 1 point, whilst 'D' have to intercept and attack the ball back to top to get 1 point. First team to 6 wins, give feedback and change roles.
CPs, Communication, Body angles, Decision making, Timing

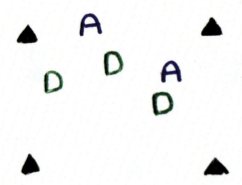

Conditioned game: Treasure Chest
'A' attack the ball to hit the spots to gain 1 point, once they have hit that spot it moves into the circle. 'D' aim is to stop 'A' hitting circle edge, if they intercept, they play the ball into the centre third to put one of the 'A's spots back on the circle edge. Play for 5mins then give feedback and repeat.

Flip the spots to the transverse line for 'D' to attack the ball out and 'A' to defend and then attack to goal for a point.

Defensive team with the most spots left wins.
CPs, Communication, Everyone doing their job, Strong body angles

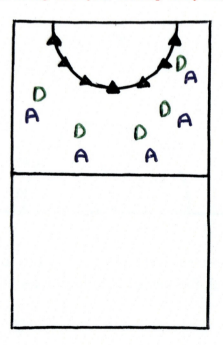

Half court:
Focus on dictating high and wide

Cool down/Feedback:
Question: What is our defensive strategy as a unit?

Samantha Griffin

Decision Making: Possession under pressure and fatigue

Aim: Being able to make good decisions under pressure

Warm up: Player led

1. Activation
2. Dynamic
3. Speed
4. Ball

Time challenge: Drive and clear drill, complete time targets before moving on, work in centre third, 2 teams. If the first team achieves 30secs the second team them become attack.
30secs
1 min
1.30 mins
2 mins
(Every failed attempt sprint to goal line and back, attackers utilise this time)
CPs, Forward drives, Release points, Reading off, Commitment, Communication

Back line out: Play 6x balls from the back, no defence, rotate players on after 6
Should have minimum of 3x plays from the back line. If 'D' brings ball high – C clears, WA comes through- key is reading off.

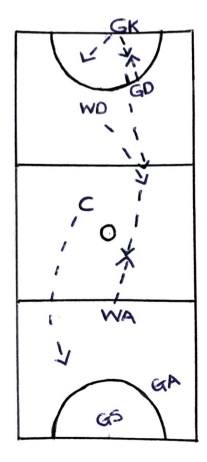 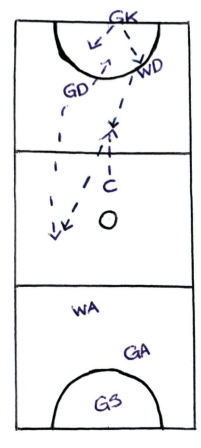 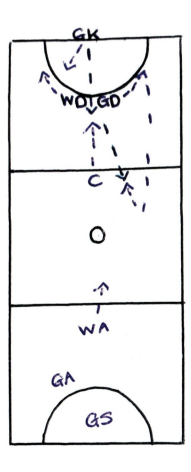

Progression: Add Defenders

CPs, Channels balanced, Reading off, Commit, Communicate

Live ball:

Half court D v A; drop the ball into play in random places for both A + D

See how they react and read off, quickly transitioning

Play 3 each then break down, question

CPs, Angles, reaction, decision making

Match Play:

Conditions:

1. 'A'- always take C unless 'D' turns the ball
2. 55-55 1 min left our centre
3. 55-55 30 secs left, defence back line (attack need to turn)
4. 56-55 winning 1 min left, our centre
5. 56-55 losing 1 min left, our centre

Change so that each team play both parts.

CPs, recap our CPA strategies

1- staggered start

2- screen

3- off the line, 'D' receives 1st phase

Cool down/Feedback

Samantha Griffin

Passing

Aim: Decision making with passing

Warm up: Player led

1. Activation
2. Dynamic
3. Speed
4. Ball

Drill 1: Set up in a square pass right until coach calls change, then pass left. When coach blows the whistle break out into pairs to complete 20 single hand passes with right hand if the whistle went whilst passing right, pass left if whistle went whilst pass left.

CPs, Single hand release, Accuracy, Timing, Communication

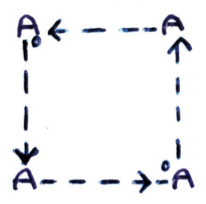

Drill 2: Set up in a square two players at the top start with the ball, both pass diagonally at the same time, the next two players both pass right, repeat for 20 passes. Change to pass diagonally to left

Progression: Start by passing diagonal to right, coach shouts change, players change to diagonal to left.

CPs, Single hand release, Accuracy, Timing, Communication

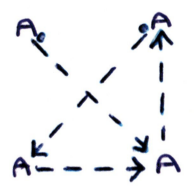

Conditioned Game: Closing in

'A' must make 20 passes in whole third, 15 in half, 10 in a quarter to gain 1 point. If 'D' intercept they become 'A'. First team to 3 points wins and ends the game.

CPs, Communication, Decision making, Definite drives, Timing

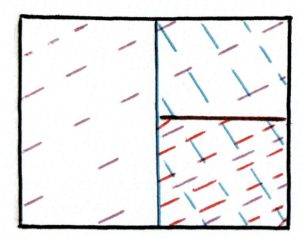

Match Play:

Condition: If a player makes a bad pass moves off the court and out the game until they have completed 3 burpees

Cool down/Feedback

Overloading the Attack

Aim: To put attack under pressure and promote successful decision making

Warm up: Player led

1. Activation
2. Dynamic
3. Speed
4. Ball

Drill 1: Attacking pyramid
'A' starts in the square with 'F' at the top and 'D' scattered around the outside.
'A' works for 3 passes with 0 defence
'A' works for 3 passes with 1 defender
'A' works for 3 passes with 2 defenders
'A' works for 3 passes with 3 defenders
If 'A' loses the ball at any point they begin the pyramid again. To challenge players, work up and down the pyramid
CPs, Commit to drive, Body angles, Ball placement, Decisions

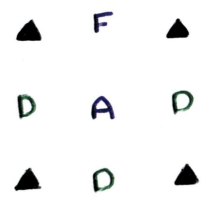

Conditioned Game: Attack v Defence
Split teams into positions WA/GA/GS attackers, GD/WD/GK defenders
'A1' must make 5 passes in centre third before attacking to goal, can use 'A2' when gaining depth.
If they score 'A1' get 1 point. If they lose the ball, they exit the court and 'A2' attempt to score.
'D1' must stay within the centre third and 'D2' stay within the goal third. Each pair gets 4 attempts at scoring. Repeat with 'D' completing the same starting at the back line to the transverse line.
Pair with the most points wins.
CPs, Definite drives, Ball placement, Communication

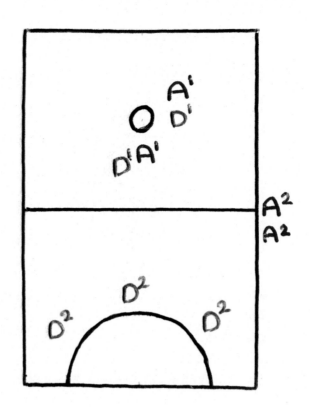

Match Play:

Condition: Add an extra defender in each third

Cool down/Feedback

GS Session

Required: GS, a defender (could be an object), Feeder could be the coach if solo session.

Aim: To develop a variety of ways for the GS to be available in the circle, as well as shooting under pressure/fatigue.

Warm Up: Cut the cake with varied dynamic movements.

Shooting:
20x goals from different places
20x goals stepping onto right leg
20x goals stepping onto left leg
Question: When might you need to step onto one leg in a match? (To get away from a 3ft mark, get closer to the post if no defender in front.)

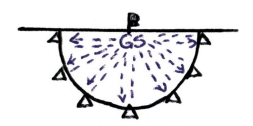

Holding GS:
1. T-hold to protect the back space
Create a T on the defender by putting one side of your body (shoulder down to foot) in the centre of 'D's back. Stay strong with your body without pushing on the defender. The other side of your body should be in line with the post, use that arm to signal for a ball. Make sure you are holding high in the circle so you have room to take the ball, do not come off the hold until the ball is above your head, land on your closest foot to the post. Ensure your body angle is open to the ball and the post, during a game you will need to keep your feet moving to adjust your angle.
Repeat x 6, then move the ball, complete 3 sets
CPs, Body angle, Strong body position, Footwork, Timing, Vision

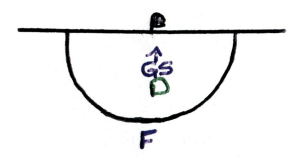

2. Front hold

Set up in-front of the defender and in line with the ball. Use your back to protect the space and prevent your defender from coming around you. As the ball is released step forward to meet it, if you feel your defender is coming around your left, step with your left leg to protect the space. Repeat x 6, then move the ball, complete 3 sets

CPs, Body angle, Strong body position, Footwork, Timing, Vision

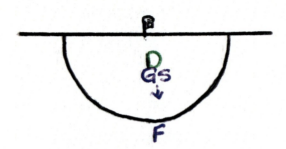

3. Changing holds

Start on with your T hold, when the feeder has not released the ball straight away come off the hold and pop forward in front of your defender. You need to be able to do this if the defender has managed to get around you. Repeat x 6 then change to starting on the front and changing to the T.

CPs, Body angle, Strong body position, Footwork, Timing, Vision

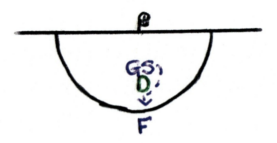

Conditioned Game: GS will start by shooting one shot, catch her rebound then pass out to 'F' and immediately set up where they want the next ball, they will need to react to 'F' if they have not given her the first time ball, once receives GS shoots again whilst 'F' changes position around the circle. Repeat until GS makes 6 successful goals. Complete 4 sets.

Shooting under fatigue/pressure: GS needs to shoot 5 consecutive goals, complete 30secs of sprinting, repeat x 4. If the GS misses at any point begins again from set 1. Can choose to bank sets but must shoot consecutive within the set. Adapt to the GS you are working with.

Cool down/Feedback

Effective Warm Up

RAMP warm up

Raise: Increase muscle temperature, core temperature, blood flow, muscle elasticity and neural activation.

Activate: Engage the muscles in preparation for the session.

Mobilize: Focus on movement patterns which will be used during the session.

Potentiate: Gradually increasing the stress on the body in preparation for the session.

Fab Five:
1. Glute Bridge
2. Hip elevated leg lifts 5x each side
3. Single leg groiner into hamstring stretch
4. Alternating leg leaps
5. Three jumps and a 90-degree turn
Complete 5 reps on each exercise

Dynamic movement: All players have a netball or tennis ball moving around within the court. When the coach shouts numbers the players apply the action, coach will also call a change in dynamic movement:
1. Throw the ball up and clap 3x before catching
2. Move the ball around the body whilst moving
3. Figure of 8 with the ball between the legs
Dynamic movement: High knees, Heal flicks, Side steps, Grapevine, High skips

Game: Post ball, split the group into two teams. Teams aim to score a point by hitting the post, can only attempt to hit the post when they have landed the ball on the circle edge, no one aloud inside the circle. Netball rules apply, first team to five points wins.

Competition: Split into teams, set up a line of 4 cones for each team with a ball, placed in line with the centre circle. Each cone has a number, coach calls numbers players must hit the numbers in order whilst going back to the line in-between each one. Once they have completed the number sequence, race to get the ball and hold above their head. Repeat until each player completes 4 attempts. Team with the most points at the end win and set a forfeit.

Acknowledgements

Thank you to Lisa Ritchie and Gayle Bacon for their unwavering support. Thank you to my assistant coaches Abi Hymas, Corey McGlynn and Millie van Nierop. Thank you to the committee, players, and parents at Charnwood Rutland Netball Club for always supporting me with every goal I set the club.

Thank you also to my family and friends for their constant support, especially when I am living on the netball court.

Samantha Griffin